CHANGING ENGLISH PRIMARY EDUCATION
retrospect and prospect

Edited by Colin Richards

Professor of Education, St. Martin's College
Honorary Professor of Education University of Warwick

Trentham Books

Stoke on Trent, UK and Sterling, USA

Trentham Books Limited

Westview House	22883 Quicksilver Drive
734 London Road	Sterling
Oakhill	VA 20166-2012
Stoke on Trent	USA
Staffordshire	
England ST4 5NP	

First published 2000

British Library Cataloguing-in-Publication Data
A catalogue record for this book is available from the British Library

1 85856 237 6

Designed and typeset by Trentham Print Design Ltd., Chester and printed in Great Britain by Cromwell Press Ltd., Wiltshire.

CHANGING ENGLISH PRIMARY EDUCATION
retrospect and prospect

Contents

This book is dedicated to the memory of Alan Blyth
— scholar, liberal, humanist, Christian and
a true friend to primary education

AGES, MYTHS AND TEACHER AUTONOMY:
changing English primary education
Colin Richards

A t the beginning of the twenty-first century primary education in England faces fundamental challenges to its assumptions, its policies and its practices. The government is attempting to 'modernise' (its term) primary education and to redefine the nature of primary professionalism. It is important that all those with a vital interest in primary education – teachers, students, governors and parents – have a sense of what has been achieved over the last thirty years and have a view of what might be or should be achieved in the future (and at what possible cost).

The contributors to this book provide both a retrospective and a prospective perspective on key areas such as teaching and learning, assessment, curriculum, management, professional development, special needs, early years, inspection, the performance culture and teacher professionalism. For the most part their chapters are up-dated versions of papers first published in the journal Education 3-13. They include many of England's leading writers on primary education such as Andrew Pollard, Maurice Galton, Geoff South-worth, Colin Conner, Marion Dadds, Ann Lewis, Marion Dowling, Norman Thomas, Denis Hayes and Jim Campbell. They are all friends and 'fellow-travellers' in the field of primary education, all seeking throughout their professional lifetimes to increase their own and others' understanding of this fascinating, but still undervalued, phase of education.

Their insights provide a very significant contribution to discussion of policy, theory and practice in contemporary primary education. Their reflections on developments and trends present a considered, balanced evaluation of where primary education is and where it has come from, to set alongside the 'myopic' version of recent developments provided in government green papers, discussion documents and annual reports. The contributions to the book illustrate the complexity of the issues facing primary teachers – much more complex than ex cathedra pronouncements, 'snapshot' inspection judgements or official 'sound bites' can illuminate, and reinforce the importance of taking a long-term view, both retrospectively and prospectively.

This editorial introduction attempts to put the contributions into an historical context by offering a brief sketch of the recent history of primary education in terms of three organising ideas, 'ages', 'myths' and 'autonomy' and to offer a glimpse of the future.

In looking back (with a rose-tinted perspective?) the period 1965-74 was an age of excitement. There were of course very real problems facing primary schools: classes very large by current standards; high turnover of staff; difficulties of teacher recruitment; the vestiges of the eleven-plus; and a backlog of poor buildings including new-style open-plan schools. Yet despite these problems there was a sense of optimism within the system – captured in the upbeat style and messages of the Plowden Report. Like the rest of the educational system, primary education was expanding in terms of numbers of pupils, increases in resources and rising public and professional expectations. Things were getting better and would continue to do so, or so we thought. There was a sense of freedom (coupled with anxiety) over the removal of the restrictions on teacher initiative following the demise (in many areas) of selection at eleven. Imaginative teachers were beginning to show what primary-aged children were capable of, given appropriate encouragement and support. The curriculum was in a state of flux. The basic staples of 'reading, writing and number' remained the heart of the curriculum but both English and mathematics were being reinterpreted and curriculum development in other areas, especially science and French, was also being promoted. There was a flowering of the arts in primary schools which hadn't been witnessed before or since. For a time it appeared that there would at long last be a much-needed expansion in nursery education. There arose the myth of a primary school revolution – founded to some degree on highly innovative practice in a small minority of schools but essentially the result of wishful thinking on the part of some child-centred educationists and of what would later come to be called, 'media-hype'. Though mythical, these ideas added to the sense of interest and anticipation in working in a system where the children, the teachers and the system itself were full of un-realised possibilities. Teachers enjoyed (albeit often anxiously) licensed autonomy; they were trusted by politicians and parents alike to take professional decisions about both the content of the curri-culum and the way it should be taught and assessed. As Marion Dadds' chapter explicitly acknowledges, this was a formative period in the professional development of some of the book's contributors.

The period 1974-88 was very different; the most severe economic crisis since before the Second World War put paid to the heady optimism of continued expansion and of lightly licensed teacher autonomy. It was an age of disillusionment – with the social-demo-cratic consensus, with the state of the British economy, with the condition of the public services, with the contribution of the educa-tion system, with the quality of primary education and with the work of primary school teachers. The heady rhetoric of the 1972 white paper, A Framework for Expansion, sounded very hollow indeed just a few years later as contraction, rather than expansion, became the order of the day. The many casualties included nursery education, as Marion Dowling points out. Government became increasingly con-cerned about, and with, the workings of the educational system including primary schools. Through populist rhetoric in the tabloid press, parental anxiety with primary education was fuelled. National surveys of both primary and secondary schools revealed an inevitable gap between professional rhetoric and practice. All these factors, within and external to the education system, helped establish a dominant myth of decline, especially of declining standards. Schools had to cope with ever more stringent contraction – of resources, of pupils, and of political and parental expectations. There was a loss of professional self-confidence and direction in the face of continuing criticism despite the fact that there was no reasonably objective or substantial evidence of the decline in standards cited by critics of primary schools. Teachers exercised monitored autonomy as central and local government developed policies for the curriculum and LEAs tried to monitor and influence practice in individual schools.

The period 1988-97 could be characterised as the age of regulation. The stirrings of governmental involvement in the content and process of education, begun in the previous period, were replaced by strong intervention especially in the areas of curriculum and assessment. For the first time since 1897, English primary schools were required to follow a detailed, codified, state-imposed curriculum with a large number of attainment targets and detailed programmes of study. For the first time since the abolition of payment by results, a national system of assessment was introduced, and then modified and re-modified over successive years. Colin Conner's contribution captures some of the changes in assessment policy and practice. Government ministers and their agents (both 'wise' and 'unwise' men, rarely women!) intervened more and more directly in the debate about the appropriate kind of teaching needed to 'deliver' the objectives of the national curriculum. Far from deregulating the education system the government of the day engaged in ever-more detailed regulation, circumscribing the limits of professional autonomy still further. The effects of these interventions on teachers' working conditions and sense of professionalism are cogently illustrated by both Jim Campbell and Denis Hayes. Regulated teacher autonomy replaced monitored autonomy. The instigation of a national cycle of inspection was an indirect way of regulating the system – policing schools' compliance with national directives and limiting high-risk experimentation with either content or process. As Norman Thomas points out, this 'new-style' inspection represented a radical departure in policy, practice and assumptions from the HMI 'system' it largely replaced. The myth of low standards, especially in reading, writing, number knowledge and the skills of calculation, was cited to justify ever tighter control and regulation through an inspection system increasingly focused on those areas and on a politically sponsored teaching methodology, with which demoralised teachers were willing to conform, at least for the purpose of surviving their inspections. The evidence cited for these supposedly low standards was at worst very suspect and at best far from conclusive.

The period we are currently experiencing began with the election of the New Labour government in 1997. That government claimed to 'hit the ground running' and has continued ever since to 'parachute' in initiative after initiative. Primary education is now experiencing an age of domination. Far from restoring (albeit in a more accountable form) initiative and freedom to experiment in the primary sector, central government has intervened ever more directly and sharply in relation to primary curriculum, pedagogy and assessment, as the contributions of Colin Richards and Denis Hayes illustrate. It has introduced a national literacy strategy which is far more detailed and prescriptive than the national curriculum orders ever were. Its numeracy strategy provides rather more 'degrees of freedom' but only relative to its literacy equivalent. It has produced detailed national schemes of work for other subjects which, though non-statutory, have considerable official backing for their implementation. It has set early learning goals for under-sixes. It has prescribed the teaching methods to be used in literacy and numeracy in a way that is dangerously close to breaking the law as laid down in the 1988 Education Reform Act. It has made a fetish of national testing – treating it as the measure by which primary schools are to be judged – and failing to recognise (at least publicly) its shortcomings, both technical and educational. It has failed to curb the excesses of Ofsted and to understand the limitations of its evidence so clearly expressed by Norman Thomas. It has used that organisation to re-inforce the domination of the measurable and gradable as the expression of educational standards and quality. It is attempting to change the whole culture of primary teaching towards what Jim Campbell calls the 'secularisation' of teaching in a performance culture. Its performance model of education has been based on what Andrew Pollard and Maurice Galton characterise as an inadequate model of learning – a model which also fails to do justice to the complexities of children's special needs so clearly delineated by Ann Lewis.

It is pursuing the myth of modernisation but paradoxically in a way more reminiscent of the nineteenth century than of the twenty-first. Modernisation is to be achieved through a form of educational totalitarianism which is 'zero tolerant of dissent' and which treats criticism as indicative of vested interests in 'old education' which need to be swept away or ignored. It claims to be basing its prescriptions for primary education on 'proven best practice' (defined officially) which it believes can almost instantly be installed in the system given enough money, scripted training and glossy materials. It offers teachers rhetorical autonomy; in principle they are free to opt out of national initiatives but at their peril given policing by Ofsted and by LEA officials with a very anxious eye on both school and LEA targets. In Marion Dadds' memorable phrase teachers are increasingly having to react to 'national hand claps'.

What of the future? Each of the contributors provides a speculative glimpse in relation to their areas of interest; some,such as Geoff Southworth, are more upbeat than others.

To finish on an optimistic note, once the national targets have been met (as they will be), once the moral panic over standards has passed (albeit temporarily), once our position in the international league tables has improved (before they are discredited as bogus), the government might reconsider its stance towards the teaching profession, whether 'secularised' or not. .Who knows ? As Norman Thomas wishes, it might even usher in an age of emancipation where well-educated teachers are encouraged and trusted by government to exploit their own and their pupils' imaginative and creative potential, albeit within a framework of national expectations and accountabilities.Teachers might be able to exercise re-licensed autonomy in order to foster children's multiple intelligences and understandings required to take advantage of the 'information-rich', 'opportunity-rich' world available to them as children, let alone as future adults. The myth of a primary school revolution might then have more substance than its equivalent 40 years before.

Learning and Teaching

TOWARDS A NEW PERSPECTIVE ON CHILDREN'S LEARNING?

Andrew Pollard

Introduction

In this paper I will suggest that recent English education policy has been influenced by external, economic and political factors, rather than founded on a valid understanding of how children's learning actually takes place. I will argue that the 'performance' model of education, which has dominated the 1990s, is inadequate in terms of its implied model of learning. I will review socio-cultural theory and propose it as a more valid conceptualisation. However, at present, this holistic validity comes at a significant cost in terms of complexity and I will present the tension between the performance and socio-cultural models in terms of some key 'dilemmas'. At some point in the future, I believe that the technocratic confidence of the performance model will begin to collapse. An important task for researchers and practitioners is therefore to prepare a more secure alternative.

Competition, performance, policy and practice

International economic interdependence increasingly undermines the capacity of national governments to control their particular economies – and at the same time generates severe anxieties about national competitiveness. Thus, in recent years and across the whole of the UK, we have experienced an enormous increase in the political attention paid to education, as successive governments have striven to address the competitiveness agenda. Irrespective of the beliefs, expertise and interests of teachers, education has become an area in which governments can present themselves as 'looking to the future' and as 'acting decisively' in the national interest.

The 'performance model' of education in the UK, which has been developed with remarkable continuity between recent Conservative and Labour governments, has defined educational discourse and focused professional attention in ways that articulate with competitiveness. Thus we have the language of curriculum delivery, attainment, targets, competence, appraisal, inspection, etc. Teachers and schools, we are told, must perform more 'effectively'. For primary education in particular, this must be achieved by raising pupil attainments in the basics of English and mathematics. The pressure of the performance model thus ultimately comes to bear on the expectations that are made of pupils.

Of course, there are echoes of the old elementary school system in relation to this narrow basic curriculum, but teachers certainly do not now characterise pupils as passive recipients of knowledge and instruction. Indeed, the continuing influence of constructivism sustains a commitment to pupils as active learners who 'make sense' of their experiences. A significant professional development therefore, achieved despite years of simplistic derision of 'child-centred' methods, is that the role of the teacher has been re-conceptualised as 'assisting performance' through appropriate direct instruction. The use of the term 'appropriate' is crucial here, for it denotes the application of professional judgement in the cognitive and motivational matching of children and new tasks.

At the end of the twentieth century therefore, English primary educators can be seen as managing a tension between two forms of discourse. The public statements of politicians and the media are often assertively categoric and simplistic – and have unfortunately been reinforced regularly by Her Majesty's Chief Inspector for Schools. On the other hand, the educationalist discourse of committed teachers has become defensively organised and reflects practical struggles in the difficult circumstances of classrooms and schools as well as responses to debates and 'moral panics' of the moment. Teachers continue to be creative in responding to new demands whilst seeking to retain their educational principles, but the introduction of hard-edged, performance systems and structures does appear to be gradually changing concepts, taken-for-granted assumptions and ways of thinking. This, of course, can be seen as the product of a sophisticated exercise of power. Thus systems, processes and relationships are created that lead people to conceptualise 'reality' in particular ways. Perception, understanding and even 'common sense' become defined in terms of a new hegemony. One element of this is the explicit concern with international economic competitiveness, whilst a second maintains tacit and unproblematised assumptions about how children are deemed to learn.

Through its systems of curriculum and pedagogy, the discourse of performance assumes that there are sufficient continuities in how children learn on which to base valid prescriptions. Thus it becomes possible to set out the detailed contents and processes of a 'literacy hour' or a 'numeracy hour'. The discourse of performance further asserts legitimacy because of its universal and 'objective' application. Implicitly, it assumes that there is sufficient homogeneity in pupil circumstances and learning potential to make valid assessments and comparisons. Such comparisons, it is assumed, can be built up from the performance of individual pupils, taking the attainment of each child as the basic unit of analysis. The claims of universalism, measurement and individual achievement are thus clear and strong – and even educational researchers can now, it seems, be selectively enlisted to demonstrate 'what works'.

However, what if there are weaknesses in the validity of the underlying conception of learning? What if there has been a consistent oversimplification of educational issues by policy-makers, so that policies do not recognise complexities and dilemmas that are actually endemic? What if social circumstances are actually very significant in school performance, or if the commitment of teachers and headteachers is undermined by the march of the system? More radically and constructively, what happens if we start from somewhere else – from a focus on learning per se?

I make no claim at this point to be able to offer a complete or perfectly-honed alternative perspective, but I want to highlight some issues which are of undeniable significance and which are certainly underplayed at present. My thinking about this derives from research at the interface of sociology and psychology, and constitutes a socio-cultural approach to learning.

A socio-cultural approach to learning

Socio-cultural psychology has been influenced considerably by Vygotsky (1978), and three core themes can be identified in his work. I will review these, and then draw on Bruner's The Culture of Education (1996) to highlight two further themes that are of particular significance for the modern application of the approach. For each of these five themes, I will provide a few illustrative examples of relevant research.

First, there is an emphasis on understanding learning developmentally – in 'genetic' terms. This approach was, of course, shared with Piaget, and draws renewed attention to developmental issues, particularly in relation to the learning of young children (Cole, 1992). Physical development, as established long ago by Tanner (1961), also remains of great significance in relation to the fulfilment, or otherwise, of biological potential. And biological factors are becoming increasingly well understood, both in terms of genetic variations and in terms of the neurological functioning of the brain (Greenfield, 1997; Claxton, 1997).

Second, the approach draws attention to the social origins of mental functioning – emphasising the ways in which intellectual capacity is intimately connected to social activity (Werstch and Tulviste, 1996; John-Steiner, 1997). Vygotsky analysed how ways of thinking are modelled in social relations and activities, before becoming internalised and available for more independent thought. Similarly, the concept of the 'zone of proximal development' emphasises the role of a more knowledgeable other (teacher, parent, peer) in providing instruction to 'scaffold' and extend a learner's understanding beyond the level of which he or she is capable alone. Tharp and Gallimore (1988) and Mercer (1995) have provided excellent studies of such processes within schools. The classic book on young children learning in interaction with their parents by Tizard and Hughes

(1984) is being complemented by more work on the importance of family and other relationships (e.g. Dunn, 1993). Among the best resources here is a new MA course from the Open University, entitled Child Development in Families, Schools and Society (ED840).

The third core theme concerns mediation, and the processes by which thought is influenced by 'tools' and 'signs'. Of course, the development of human capabilities has been closely linked to the use of physical tools and technologies. However, socio-cultural theory draws attention to the ways in which the availability and use of the tools of a society actually shape and form cognition. A telling modern illustration of this argument concerns the use of computer tools, with both hardware (such as the mouse, joystick or micro-phone) and software (such as wordprocessors, spreadsheets, data-bases and simulators) enabling and structuring new practices and thought processes. The importance of the mediation of thought through sign systems is even more marked. Thus the symbolic logics of languages, scripts, numeric and algebraic systems, art, texts, dia-grams and other forms of representation shape and make possible our thoughts. Such tools and sign systems are the products of socio-cultural history, and are appropriated and internalised by individuals as they develop within their societies (Rogoff and Lave (1984), Wertsch (1991). Some interesting concepts have been developed to describe these processes. For instance, there is the notion of a 'dis-tributed intelligence' that exists within our culture, and is embodied in a range of 'cognitive tools'. Lave and Wenger (1991) argue that 'communities of practice' develop in everyday social relationships in which particular ways of knowing are embedded. New learners engage in 'legitimate, peripheral participation' before they become enculturated and knowledgeable within the social practices. At another level completely, anthropological and comparative studies have demonstrated how different cultures embed and reproduce particular ideas and social practices. Thus detailed inter-cultural case studies of children's upbringing are becoming available, such as those of Richards and Light (1986) and Whiting and Edwards (1988).

Bruner (1996) has built on this approach in his discussion of the 'culture of education', and our fourth theme is derived from this work. Bruner begins by affirming the Vygotskian position by seeing 'reality' as the 'product of meaning-making shaped by traditions and by a culture's toolkit of ways of thought' (p.19), but he then highlights education as a key institutional process whereby a society shares existing knowledge and negotiates new forms. As he puts it, educational institutions 'do the culture's serious business' (p.30). This serious business is not, however, without some risk to individuals, and Bruner highlights an 'unpredictable mix of coercion and voluntarism' within schooling systems. The institutional culture, social processes and micro-politics of each school are also vital here (Hoyle, 1982; Ball, 1987). Indeed, in some of my own longitudinal work with Ann Filer, we have tracked the ways in which the 'strategic biographies' of children are affected by their annual cycles of social experience as they move through school careers (Pollard and Filer, 1999). Their particular mix of success and failure, opportunity and frustration, reflects the social construction of 'ability' within the school and is crucial to their self-belief as learners.'

Finally, the 'risk' to individuals draws attention to 'the phenomenon of self', which Bruner characterises as 'perhaps the single most universal thing about human experience' (1996: 35). Whilst there is cultural variation in the ways in which self-esteem is experienced, Bruner asserts that 'any system of education that diminishes the school's role in nurturing its pupils' self-esteem fails at one of its primary functions' (38). In summary, he argues that 'education must help those growing up in a culture to find an identity within that culture. Without it, they stumble in their effort after meaning' (42). This is a key argument in The Social World of Children's Learning (Pollard with Filer, 1996), a book in which I attempted to demonstrate the significance of social influences on the self-confidence and approaches to new learning challenges of children from age four to seven.

Here then, we have an approach to learning that attempts to envision the links between history, culture, language, symbols, thought, relationships, social organisations, activity, biological development, self, identity and even (if we follow Bruner) the 'meaning of life'!

Dilemmas, and a task

The socio-cultural model is impressive in its range, depth and vision. It aspires to a holism that will resonate with the tacit understandings and experienced knowledge of everyday life. However, some may say that it is foolhardy to attempt to embrace so many factors, and may feel much more secure, with the clear-cut and technical logic of the performance model. I have some sympathy for this view at this stage in the development of the socio-cultural perspective. Research is still at a creative and formative point, with many leads and directions being followed, and it will take time for a more integrated set of tenets to become established and presented in forms that are likely to make a direct impact on education policy. Nevertheless, in my opinion, this is exactly what we will see in future decades as the performance model begins to disappoint and as alternative conceptions become more coherent.

However, it is instructive to consider the particular strengths of the perspectives, and dilemma analysis offers a tidy way of doing this. There appears to be a basic dilemma between the multifaceted attempt at holistic validity offered by the socio-cultural model and the practical construction of a structured and measurable education system that is underpinned by the performance model. There are echoes here of the classic researchers' dilemma between validity and reliability. When validity is prioritised, the complexity of relevant phenomena may become unmanageable, but when reliability is emphasised, research may fail to produce findings of meaningful significance. Among researchers, a constructive tension between the twin priorities of validity and reliability is generally accepted, and this gradually leads to innovation and improvement in quality. Sadly, the recent climate of educational debate has not been so constructive, for the systematic prosecution of the performance model has been linked to a discourse of derision and a confrontational approach towards those with reservations or alternative perspectives. If those who are not 'for' are simply deemed to be 'against', then the powerful may prevail – but tragically, they also deny themselves an opportunity to learn.

Nevertheless, because of the range and basic validity to which the socio-cultural model aspires, policies that are consistent with it do break through from time to time. For instance, during the 'Year of Reading' attempts were made to enlist companies, communities and the media in activities to support literacy activity. Whilst the overall initiative was highly managed, it nevertheless recognised the significance of embedding literacy within social relations and harnessing the efforts of existing social institutions. Even more radical initiatives might have been attempted if the full implications of Barton and Hamilton's mould-breaking book on 'local literacies' (1998) were followed up. Similarly, the recent efforts of the Social Exclusion Unit to develop provision on large estates suffering from multiple disadvantages also shows awareness of the holistic conditions that affect learning and development. In particular, it suggests that, at least somewhere in Whitehall, there is recognition that social development needs more than the naming, blaming, shaming and failing of schools. The Demos publication on 'learning beyond the classroom' (Bentley, 1998) is encouraging in this context. But such initiatives seem haphazard, and do not appear to reflect sustained, strategic awareness of the management of the key dilemmas.

Some apparent dilemmas that are posed by the performance and socio-cultural models are: Goals that are clear and measurable – or potentially diffuse, long-term or even ephemeral; Roles which are specific and delimited – or interdependent and integrated; Relationships of authority – or those which call for multiple partnerships; Control that is centralised – or relatively devolved; Curricula that provide consistent entitlements – or are responsive to particular needs; Practices that are homogeneous – or reflect the complexities of modern cultures and traditions.

The overall position may seem to contrast 'precise' with 'fuzzy', and there is an element of truth in this. However, in my view, the perspectives can also be contrasted in the gross simplification of educational processes that the performance model embodies and the attempt to work from more complex and valid understandings in the case of socio-cultural approaches. Of course the latter is more difficult, and of course politicians cannot wait in the optimistic hope that researchers will arrive (uniquely) with new 'truths' about learning and how best to facilitate it. However, we should not forget that thoughtful and aware parents and teachers have always understood many of these issues, even if they may not have been easy to articulate analytically. In this context, we could all benefit from more recognition of the inherent difficulty of both understanding learning and improving our education system – and it would be good to conceptualise the shared task, and work together.

References

Ball, S. (1987) The Micropolitics of Schooling, Routledge: London.

Barton, D. and Hamilton, M. (1998) Local Literacies: Reading and Writing in One Community, Routledge: London.

Bentley, T. (1998) Learning Beyond the Classroom, Routledge: London.

Bruner, J. S. (1996) The Culture of Education, Harvard University Press: Cambridge, MA.

Claxton, G. (1997) Hare Brain, Tortoise Mind, London: Fourth Estate.

Cole, M. (1992) 'Culture in development', in Developmental Psychology, LEA: Hillsdale, NJ.

Dunn, J. (1993) Young Children's Close Relationships, Sage: Newbury Park, Calif.

Greenfield, S. (1997) The Human Brain: A Guided Tour, London: Weidenfeld and Nicolson.

Hoyle, E. (1982) 'The micropolitics of educational organisations', Education, Management and Administration, No 10, pp 87-98.

John-Steiner, V. (1997) Notebooks of the Mind: Explorations of Thinking, Oxford University Press: New York.

Lave, J. and Wenger, E. (1991) Situated Learning: Legitimate Peripheral Participation, Cambridge University Press: New York.

Mercer, N. (1995) The Guided Construction of Knowledge, Clevedon: Multilingual Matters.

Pollard, A. and Filer, A. (1999) The Social World of Pupil Career, Cassell: London.

Pollard, A. with Filer, A. (1996) The Social World of Children's Learning, Cassell: London.

Richards, M. and Light, P. (1986) Children of Social Worlds, Polity Press: Cambridge.

Rogoff, B. and Lave, J. (1984) Everyday Cognition: Its Development in Social Context, Harvard University Press: Cambridge, MA.

Tanner, J. M. (1961) Education and Physical Growth, University of London: London.

Tharp, R. and Gallimore, R. (1988) Rousing Minds to Life, Cambridge University Press: New York.

Tizard, B. and Hughes, M. (1984) Young Children Learning, Fontana: London.

Vygotsky, L. S. (1978) Mind in Society, Harvard University Press: Cambridge, MA.

Wertsch, J. V. (1991) Voices of the Mind, Harvard University Press: Cambridge, MA.

Wertsch, J. V. and Tulviste, P. (1996) 'L. S. Vygotsky and contemporary developmental psychology', in Daniels, H. ed. An Introduction to Vygotsky, Routledge: London.

Whiting, B. B. and Edwards, C. P. (1988) Children of Different Worlds, Harvard University Press: Cambridge, MA.

DANCING IN *OKLAHOMA*:
How to compete effectively in
the twenty-first century
Maurice Galton

I began life as a researcher over twenty years ago when I began observing science lessons in Leicestershire comprehensive schools. From there I joined forces with Professor Brian Simon to carry out what still today remains the largest systematic survey of primary classroom practice. The ORACLE (Observational Research and Classroom Learning Evaluation) study led to other research, first on group work and then on the curriculum of small rural schools and their attempts to implement the National Curriculum during the early nineties. Finally I have recently replicated part of the original ORACLE studies including the move of pupils from primary to secondary school. In my lifetime as a researcher I have probably been into more primary classrooms up and down the country than all but the most industrious Ofsted[1] inspectors.

I have to report that my general impression, once you penetrate below the surface of the classroom, is of little significant change. In the first year of secondary school science lessons are much the same as they were during ORACLE, and indeed much the same as when I studied the subject at school. Take, for example, a typical description of an early science lesson during the first term after transfer to a 10-14 school. The field note, compiled in October 1996, reads as follows:

> The lesson begins five minutes late because teachers in the various maths sets have not kept to time. Some pupils have stopped at their lockers to pack their bags so that they can go straight home after the laboratory period ends. The bags are dumped in a huge pile in the corner of the room.

Miss Mesham reminds pupils that unless they arrive on time they will not be able to do exciting experiments. Today they are going to learn about filtration. She begins by asking them for examples of filtration in the home. She mentions the word coffee but either the children all drink instant brands, use plungers, or amuse themselves by only talking about tea bags much to Miss Mesham's frustration. 'Oh you are asleep today' she tells them 'Too much dinner'.

She produces a filter funnel, demonstrates how to fold the paper, and then sends them to a cupboard to get similar apparatus and a retort stand to hold the funnel. She then points to a bottle of dirty water, tells them to fill half a beaker with it and to pour it into the filter collecting the clear liquid in a conical flask. All these objects are on the front bench clearly labelled.

The filtration experiment takes five minutes. For the rest of the lesson the class has to write up the experiment. Miss Mesham puts up an overhead with a labelled diagram and paragraphs which pupils have to copy and fill in the missing words from the list at the bottom. It reads 'We took a filter f——- and a filter p—— and stood it in the r——- stand. Then we poured the dirty l———- into the f——- and collected the r——- in a c——— flask. It was c——— etc.

At one point during the experimenting there is a slight altercation with a boy who has not put on his safety glasses.

Miss Mesham: What have I been telling you these past two weeks?
Boy pupil: But its only water. That's not dangerous.
Miss Mesham: Doesn't matter. Wear them always.
Boy pupil (mutters as Miss Mesham moves away): Stupid old bag.
Miss Mesham (turning) What did you say?
Boy: I've got to get something from my bag Miss.

The above episode is similar to other lessons on Bunsen burners, evaporation and use of thermometers, where the main objective is to introduce techniques and terminology without any reference to context. Similar results were observed by Suffolk inspectors who reported that 'early work in Year 7 was of an introductory nature involving, typically, aspects of safety and the Bunsen burner. Generally high school teachers underestimated the pupils' prior levels of attainment and particularly in relation to investigative skills' (Suffolk LEA, 1997 p2 Annex C).

Our evidence from the ORACLE replication study, however, does not paint such an attractive contrast between the investigative primary classroom and the more straightforward traditional secondary pattern. There have been changes in primary practice but these largely concern classroom organisation. Whereas in 1976 only 19 per cent of interaction took place with the whole class, this figure had risen to 35.5 per cent in 1996. In science, supposedly consisting mainly of investigations, whole-class interaction occupied over 50 per cent of the typical lesson. When one looks further at the kinds of interactions taking place then, although there is an increase overall compared to 1976, most of it consists of teachers talking at pupils. The ratio of teacher statements to teacher questions has remained almost unchanged over two decades. In 1976 it was 3.7 statements to every question. Now the ratio is 3.6 (Galton *et al.*, 1999a: 62).

Pupils still spend 71 per cent of their time not interacting with pupils or peers as against a figure of 84 per cent in 1976. This difference, however, is mainly accounted for by the pupils' silent participation during whole-class teaching as listeners. Levels of feedback, shown to be an important determinant of pupil attainment, remain remarkably stable.

Now all this is strange because for twenty years I have continually read statements from critics of primary teaching that the problem was that too few and not too many facts were being taught. When I began these classroom observations we were being told by the so called 'Black Paper' authors that 'the modern child is encouraged to read fluently and talk glibly in terms commensurate with his tender years; but the introduction to the process of hard learning and mastering what can be called the mechanics of the subject, is put off too long', leading to teachers becoming 'peripatetic advisers' (Cox and Dyson, 1969: 57).

Similar sentiments have, of course, been frequently expressed by the Chief Inspector who is keen that children 'should suspend their eagerness to criticise and learn something first' (Woodhead, 1995: 8). In this view he seems to have the support of the previous Conservative government and New Labour both in and out of office. According to Professor Reynolds, Woodhead's contributions 'have given Britain a leading edge in first-class practice' although the professor admits that it has been at a cost of 'scattering wounded bodies across the educational floor' (Observer, 25 April 1999p. 28).

So will history treat the last quarter of the twentieth century as a time when the tide of progressivism was finally turned back? Will the new millennium see a grateful Mr Blair nominate our beloved chief inspector as one of the new senators to the revised upper house of parliament? And will Mr Woodhead, rather like the vicar of Bray[2] change sides as the need arises and end up as Minister for Education in a future Conservative government (should there be another one)?

My prediction is that in the not-too-distant future the current edifice will have been dismantled among much recrimination and the chief inspector will prove an easy target on which to place most of the blame. For as Professor Reynolds (who has clearly moved around the world a bit since his fleeting visit to Taiwan for a Panorama programme) argues in his Observer article, 'his (Chris Woodhead's) diatribes against progressive methods are educationally unsound since 'helping children to learn to learn is viewed as essential by educators right across the globe'. In his peroration Professor Reynolds argues for a blending of the different methods because both are needed, each to generate different skills.

Just what that blend should be, however, is far from clear largely because, as Brian Simon has long argued, we have never had a tradition of taking pedagogy seriously (Simon, 1981, 1994). And this brings me to my title and the subject of dancing in Rogers and Hammerstein's great musical extravaganza, 'Oklahoma'.

I have always been interested in the role of the outside expert in children's learning. Visiting primary schools one is generally struck by the quality of work that results from the presence of an artist or writer in residence. One recent encounter concerned the evaluation of one of an EDSI (Education Department's Superhighways Initiative) involving video artists working with key-stage-1 pupils to produce a multimedia presentation of the family history of pupils. The quality of the work produced was such that it was exhibited at the Photographers' Gallery in London. But for my example I want to use dance and drama. The main theatre in Leicester (where I worked before moving to Homerton College, Cambridge) has always been famous for its use of children, whether in Joseph and his Amazing Technicolor Dreamcoat, or in Kipp's War (a story of wartime evacuees) or as the chorus in Greek tragedy. The director concerned has an international reputation for producing outstanding performances from amateur child actors.

But my story centres on two teenage professional dancers, hired to play cowboys in the Leicester version of Oklahoma which subsequently transferred to the Palace Theatre in London for a lengthy run. Dancers are a bit like session musicians: one week they can provide the chorus on a television variety show, the next they may be required for a commercial but if lucky they may get a place in a long running West End hit show. To progress in their career dancers need to be very flexible and quick to pick up new routines. The conventional view is they do not need to be intellectual, just quick witted so that the steps and sequences can be accomplished automatically. Generally in musical productions actors and dancers don't mix.

Not so in this production of Oklahoma. The director, the same one with the reputation for working with young children, began by explaining about the life of a cowboy. He had dancers as well as actors improvise scenes in which they branded steers and attempted to spin a rope and lasso an object. He read them accounts of life on a cattle station and discussed endlessly, or so it seemed to the dancers, problems of loneliness and so forth. The dancers became increasingly frustrated insisting that they needed to get on and practise the steps, otherwise they would not be ready by the first night of the production. 'We're not actors. We don't need all this background.' they argued. 'Just point us in the correct part of the set, start the music and we will take off.'

Their fears, however, were unfounded. On the first night critics hailed the dancing as an outstanding part of the production. Most of the credit went to the choreographer but I like to think it had more to do with the director because by teaching them to understand what it felt like to be a cowboy he enabled them to dance like cowboys. In the same way by teaching pupils to understand what it is to be a mathematician, scientist or historian, children come to think like mathematicians, scientists and historians. Psychologists refer to this kind of knowledge as metacognition, knowledge of one's cognitive processes (Alexander *et al.*, 1991). Without this knowledge it is im-

21

possible to regulate one's thought processes and engage in problem solving without help. Becoming what Lehelma and Gordon (1997) term a 'professional pupil' in order to cope with the vagaries of secondary teaching demands that pupils leave primary and middle schools 'metacognitively wise'. Whereas initially children learn to think for themselves by holding conversations with their teachers or peers, in order to regulate their own thinking they need to hold similar conversations in their own heads (Brown and Palincsar, 1986). the evidence from follow-up studies of primary children at the end of key stage 4 suggests that moving to the secondary school without this kind of knowledge is a considerable handicap (Sammons et al., 1995).

Our recent work on transfer and transition (Galton et al, 1999b) suggests that for at least 40 per cent of pupils, who score fewer marks on the same tests of basic skills twelve months after moving to the secondary school, there is a considerable problem, particularly in science where levels of motivation (as evidenced by the proportion of time on task) fall drastically after transfer. Whereas in primary school nearly 65 per cent of pupils observed were fully engaged, defined as 'on task', during at least 75 per cent of observations made during the year, at secondary level the figure was only around 35 per cent. Yet in a survey of schools, carried out for the above review, in which principals were asked what they were doing to alleviate such problems, fewer than 10 per cent had introduced any new curriculum initiative and fewer than 5 per cent any initiative to improve continuity in teaching and learning.

Elsewhere (Galton et al., 1999b) I have argued for two specific approaches. The first requires what might be termed induction courses in the first week of each school year, with the emphasis on Lehelma and Gordon's (1997) notion of pupils as professional learners. This is the equivalent of the induction for the dancers in learning to dance like cowboys. Such programmes would concentrate on helping pupils to understand the purpose of learning in certain ways rather than, as at the moment, concentrating on school rules and expected learning outcomes. Such issues as 'Why we work in groups', 'What is the purpose of different kinds of homework?' and 'How, when a teacher is looking at and commenting on a pupil's work, he or she should be looked on as a critical friend, rather than a judge of the correctness of the answer' would all be addressed. In particular, the ambiguities inherent in engaging in activities designed to promote understanding and critical thinking would be explored. In class-rooms, this ambiguity often centres on the teachers' failure to appreciate that, whereas the distinction between their role as managers of classroom behaviour and as facilitators of learning appears clear-cut, this is not true for many pupils. While the teacher's message to the class may be 'When it's about behaviour do as I say but when it's about learning do as you think, to the pupil there is uncertainty as to whether the teacher's question is designed to find out whether he or she is paying attention (behaviour) or whether he or she is capable of advanced thought (learning). In these circumstances, as the research over several decades demonstrates, pupils remain silent and let one of their peers take the risk of wrongly guessing what is going on in the mind of the teacher

Again, as argued elsewhere, changing the present approach demands school leadership based on what Williamson and Galton (1998) term consequential collegiality. This approach (based on a notion of teachers' professional development in which the stage teachers attain is marked by a shift in thinking from a deliberative mode to an intuitive, improvisational one (Berliner, 1994) demands different forms of in-service provision at different developmental stages, ranging from coaching at the deliberative stage based on reflection of other colleagues' practice to action research based on reflection of one's own performance.

At present, we know there are dips in performance as pupils move between schools (transfer) and also sometimes when pupils move up a year group within schools (transition). What we do not know is whether these relatively small annual dips in attainment are cumulative. I suspect that for a sizeable minority of pupils there are. In which case, unless we can teach these pupils to become 'meta-cognitively wise' and, metaphorically speaking, 'learn to dance like cowboys', we are building up considerable problems for ourselves. For compared to a previous era, when we were attempting to cope with industrialism with a workforce possessing low levels of literacy and numeracy, the cost of now failing to produce young adults who have 'learned how to learn' could, in the rapidly changing world of the post-traditional society of the twenty-first century, lead to levels of unemployment and consequent poverty which we have not yet dared to contemplate.

Notes

1. Ofsted is the acronym for the Office for Standards in Education, the body charged with carrying out the inspection of schools in England. Its Chief Inspector, Chris Woodhead, has been accused of hounding teachers and helping to drive down the morale of the profession by his criticisms and claims that large numbers of teachers should be dismissed from their posts.

2. The vicar of Bray was the subject of a sixteenth-century popular song. During the religious persecution of the time he regularly changed from being a Roman Catholic to a Protestant clergyman according to who was on the throne of England. The song's chorus ran 'And whatsoever king may reign still I'll be the Vicar of Bray, Sir'.

References

Alexander, P., Schallert, D. and Hare, V. (1991) 'Coming to terms; How researchers in learning and literacy talk about knowledge', Review of Educational Research, 61:3

Berliner, D. (1994) 'Expertise: the wonder of exemplary performance' in J.N. Mangieri and C, Collings (Eds) Creating Powerful Thinking in Teachers and Students: Diverse Perspectives, Fort Worth, Texas: Harcourt, Brace.

Brown, A. and Palincsar, A. (1986) Guided Cooperative Learning and Individual Knowledge Acquisition, Technical report 372, Cambridge Mass: Bolt, Bernanak and Newham Inc.

Cox, C. and Dyson, A (1969) Eds. The Fight for Education: A Black Paper, London: The Critical Quarterly Society.

Galton, M., Hargreaves, L., Comber, C. and Well, D. (1999a) Inside the Primary Classroom: 20 years On, London: Routledge

Galton, M., Gray, J. and Rudduck, J (1999b) The Impact of School Transitions and Transfers on Pupils Progress and Attainment, Research Report No RR 131, London: Department for Education and Employment.

Lehelma, E. and Gordon, T. (1997) First day in secondary school: learning to be a 'professional pupil', Educational Research and Evaluation, 3:1.

Sammons, P., Nutall. D., Cuttance, P. and Thomas, S. (1995) 'Continuity of School Effects: A longitudinal analysis of primary and secondary school effects on GCSE performance, School Effectiveness and School Improvement, 6:4.

Simon, B. (1981) 'Why no Pedagogy in England?' in Simon, B. and Taylor, W. (Eds) Education in the Eighties: The Central Issues, London: Batsford.

Suffolk LEA (1997) Building Bridges: A Report of Inspectors of Transfer at Key Stages Two and Three, Ipswich: Suffolk County Council Local Education Authority.

Williamson, J. and Galton, M. (1998) 'Building a School Culture' in Townsend, T. (Eds) The Primary School in Changing Times; The Australian Experience, London: Routledge

Woodhead, C. (1995) 'Teaching Quality: The Issues and the Evidence', in Ofsted Teaching Quality: The Primary Debate, London: Office for Standards in Education.

ENTITLEMENT OR NEO-ELEMENTARY?:
the changing English primary curriculum*

Colin Richards

The primary curriculum 1988 -98

The legal basis of the English primary curriculum remains the Education Reform Act (ERA) of 1988 and its associated regulations. While the broad framework of subjects, attainment targets, programmes of study and assessment arrangements has remained a 'given' since then, the detailed regulations governing it have been subject to many modifications, especially changes to assessment and reporting requirements. De jure the ERA does not prescribe the totality of the primary curriculum; schools have discretion, especially since the Dearing Review of 1993 (Dearing, 1993), to go beyond the national curriculum and religious education if they so wish. In the early day of its introduction there was some 'official' encouragement (from the National Curriculum Council and even from the Department of Education and Science) to make explicit provision for a range of cross-curricular themes (such as environmental education and health education) but this support was soon withdrawn as a result of 'right-wing' pressure and such issues have remained minority provision. Only with the introduction of the revised national curriculum operative from Autumn 2000 has the

---

* This chapter is a shortened updated version of Richards, C. (1999) The Primary Curriculum: past, present and future, ASPE Paper 8, Trentham Books.

government 'resurrected' the notion of cross-curricular themes in the shape of a non-statutory framework for personal, social and health education and citizenship at key stages 1 and 2 (DfEE/QCA, 1999).

Despite introducing a national curriculum, the conservative government of 1988 did not provide a rationale for the curriculum or even consider that one was desirable. The only semblance of a rationale was given in what civil servants in 1988 disparagingly called the 'motherhood and apple pie' clauses of Section 1 of the ERA, which entitled every pupil in a state school to a balanced (never defined or characterised in regulations) and broadly based (never defined) curriculum which (a) promoted the spiritual, moral, cultural, mental and physical development (never defined) of the pupils at the school and of society (never clarified); and (b) prepared such pupils for the opportunities, responsibilities and experiences of adult life (but presumably not of life as lived in the here and now!). Recently the need for an explicit statement of the aims and purposes of the school curriculum was recognised by the QCA. Such a rationale, setting out the values and aims of the school curriculum and the purposes of the national curriculum, was published as an introduction in the handbooks setting out national curriculum requirements from Autumn 2000 onwards but tellingly it remains a non-statutory element. (DfEE/QCA, 1999)

The original national curriculum could be neatly encapsulated in a formula:

$$WC = N + R + x$$

$$(\text{where } x = s + t)$$

i.e. the whole curriculum (WC) comprised the national curriculum (N) plus religious education (R) plus other components (x) including cross-curricular skills (s) and themes (t). Even before the ERA had been passed the government had decided upon a hierarchy of subjects within the curriculum. To use a football analogy appropriate at the time, the members of the 'first division' were English, mathematics and science (the latter always dangerously near to 'relegation'); as the very 'core' of the curriculum the programmes of study in these subjects were produced first, developed in most detail and made subject to national assessment arrangements. In the 'second division' were the subjects of history, geography and technology, not subject to as detailed content requirements or to national assessment. Established last of all and given the most sketchy treatment in content and assessment terms were the 'third division' subjects of art, music and physical education. Legally, religious education was not part of the national curriculum; it nevertheless had to be provided in all maintained schools. The cross-curricular themes were part of the 'non-league' provision.

Early in 1998, given the recurrent 'moral panic' over standards in numeracy and literacy, the government reorganised its curricular hierarchy into a 'premier division' consisting only of English and mathematics (with an emphasis on reading, writing and number) and a reconstituted 'first' division of science, information technology and religious education. In these divisions the current detailed requirements in the programmes of study were still mandatory on all state primary schools. All other national curriculum subjects were relegated into the lowest division where the detailed (as opposed to a token) entitlement of the national curriculum did not have to apply – unless primary schools chose to provide it. That curricular hierarchy was reproduced in the curriculum operative from Autumn 2000.

As yet, in line with the prohibitions outlined in the ERA, the government does not mandate teaching texts or materials (though those developed as a result of the national literacy and numeracy strategies are acquiring canonical status!), nor the way the curriculum is to be organised (though schools have to provide dedicated, clearly identified time each day for literacy and numeracy!), nor the teaching methods to be used (though those pretentiously and inaccurately described as 'in line with proven best practice' (DfEE, 1997b) and incorporated in government-sponsored INSET and learning materials for numeracy and literacy are being pushed very hard indeed as a new pedagogic orthodoxy!).

Integral to the current national curriculum and the government's national targets for literacy and numeracy ('doomed to success' given the political capital and drive behind them?) are the legally prescribed arrangements related to the assessment of pupils' performance, currently focusing on the original core subjects (but with ICT likely to be added before too long?). Grandiosely and unrealistically these arrangements were originally designed to serve a variety of purposes simultaneously – formative, summative, evaluative and informative. In reality, government policy originally based on the recommendations of the TGAT report (DES, 1988) proved to be far ahead of the assessment 'know how' and 'technology' available to deliver it. As a consequence the summative aspects of individual pupil assessment are now pre-eminent along with the use of national test data to compare the performance and effectiveness of apparently 'similar' 'benchmark' schools. That same disjuncture between policy aspirations and the state of assessment 'know how' and 'technology' continues to this day, with the current government failing to recognise the severe limitations of the testing regime on which it is relying to 'benchmark' schools and measure progress towards the achievement of its national targets. Despite the confident claims of Excellence in Schools (DfEE, 1997a) it is far from certain that 'We now have sound, consistent, national measures of pupil achievement for each school at each Key Stage of the National Curriculum' or that the system can adequately assess the kinds of 'rich' knowledge and skills which it claims to be able to do (see Davis, 1999 for a well-argued critique)

Has the national curriculum had a marked effect on practice? Policy and practice in primary education are inevitably loosely-coupled; mediation by individual schools and teachers undoubtedly affects the way any policy is implemented, even in the case of something as prescriptive as the national literacy strategy (Dann and Simco, 2000). Evidence from research and inspection tallied in certain respects. It was clear from both sources that after a certain amount of initial disbelief and passive resistance primary schools made determined efforts to implement national curriculum requirements; full compliance, particularly before the Dearing Review and to a lesser degree after it, proved problematic because of content overload; only a minority of schools felt able to go beyond legal requirements (Galton and Fogelman, 1997) despite Dearing's offer of 'discretion'. Tellingly, following a twenty-year period of curriculum development prior to the passing of the ERA, those provisions of the Act enabling schools to disapply aspects of the national curriculum in order to carry out educational experiments remained a 'dead letter' as far as primary education was concerned.

Research, inspection and monitoring by national agencies also demonstrated very clear weaknesses in policy formulation – content overload, especially though not only in the period 1989-93; impossibly complex assessment requirements in the early stages giving rise to dangerously simplistic and flawed ones later; considerable incoherence and lack of clarity in many of the initial statutory orders; and lack of encouragement for local experimentation and discretion.

Beyond that the research evidence was equivocal. The PACE project (Pollard et al., 1994) provided evidence of change whilst that reported by Alexander et al. (1995), Campbell and Neil (1994a, 1994b), Campbell (1997) and Plewis and Veltman (1996) suggested general continuity with previous practice rather than substantial change.

Based on a reading of HMI inspection findings prior to 1988 and of HMI/Ofsted findings thereafter, the national curriculum appeared to have brought about real, though in political terms, unspectacular change. Overall, compared with the kind of 'curriculum lottery' (Richards, 1997a) which operated prior to 1988 a more consistent curriculum entitlement was offered to children in English primary schools. Both whole-school and individual teachers' planning improved. Teachers acquired a more sophisticated, defensible view of what constituted progression and standards in the subjects they taught. Established curricular and pedagogic practices were questioned and, in many schools, partially reconstituted. In key stage 2 in particular there was a substantial shift towards more subject-based work, though a mixed economy of separate subject and topic work still operated in many schools, with topics becoming increasingly 'subject-focused' (i.e. concentrating on one subject and drawing on only a limited number of others where these are directly relevant) or 'subject-specific' (modules involving content and activities related to only one programme of study). Despite many initial reservations, by 2000 most schools had established a modus vivendi in relation to the subject basis of the national curriculum. There was a marked increase in the incidence of whole-class teaching (Galton, 1998,1999), though not to the exclusion of other forms of pupil grouping.

In general, primary-aged children had a broader curriculum than previously, broader both in terms of the subjects learnt and the range of content and activities within each subject. There was better continuity and progression in their learning, though passage across key-stage interfaces continued to have an adverse effect on pupils' progress and continuity of experience. Children's attainment was assessed rather more accurately, especially in key stage 1. Pupils' standards of attainment in subjects such as science, geography and history improved. There was no reasonably definitive evidence that in the period 1988-98 pupils' achievements in reading and number fell. What limited national curriculum test data there were were consistent with a gradual recent rise in standards.

Up to 1998, English primary schools provided one of three kinds of curriculum:

1. Many, probably the majority, 'played safe' and provided a legal entitlement curriculum (Richards, 1997b) – teaching their pupils what the ERA required (the national curriculum and locally determined religious education) but nothing beyond that i.e. not attempting to create a distinctive curriculum of their own by adding other elements. Published Ofsted inspection reports provided plentiful evidence of such curricula. To use a sartorial analogy such schools offered 'off-the-peg curricula'.

2. Some provided an enriched legal entitlement curriculum giving their pupils their legal entitlement in terms of national curriculum subjects and religious education but going beyond these to offer other elements to enrich the basic curriculum 'fare' in line with their particular interests, expertise or environment.

Some schools, for example, introduced 'new' subjects such as a modern foreign language or philosophy for children in one or more year groups. Some developed 'specialist' emphases to their curricula by offering a subject or more than one subject to a greater depth and/or range than the national curriculum required. Some devoted time to teaching cross-curricular issues such as environmental education, health education or citizenship. Some introduced programmes of personal and social development throughout the school. The more adventurous undertook a combination of these. To use the sartorial analogy, such schools provided 'tailor-made' or 'bespoke' curricula.

3. In the light of ever-increasing accountability demands, intensified, not mitigated by, government white papers; accusations (myths?) of declining standards in the 'basics'; ever-increasing emphasis on literacy and numeracy, unfavourable and ill-founded comparisons with other countries (see Galton and Morris, 1998, Broadfoot *et al.*, 2000); and an Ofsted-led curriculum focusing ever more tightly on the three original core subjects, a growing number of primary schools provided a neo-elementary curriculum: devoting more time than ever to reading, writing and number (especially those elements found in the national tests) and giving only rudimentary, superficial 'regard' to other national curriculum subjects. This kind of provision might be dubbed a 'hand-me-down curriculum'!

The primary curriculum 1998 – 2000

Following the government's announcement in January 1998 that statutory requirements for the non-core subjects were to be lifted until September 2000, primary schools adopted one of four alternative curricula:

1. an enriched reduced legal entitlement curriculum, where schools wanted to provide their own distinctive curricula and were attracted by the chance to leave out problematic elements of the programmes of study in the newly designated non-core subjects but were also aware of the need to find time beyond the literacy and numeracy 'hours' to implement the full programmes of study in English and mathematics and to meet their supposedly individually negotiated targets;

2. a legal entitlement curriculum, where schools were determined to provide broad curricula in line with the requirements of the

ERA and where they resisted the pressure to increase their emphasis on the tested subjects in the light of target-setting;

3. a reduced legal entitlement curriculum, where schools took notions of curricular breadth and balance seriously but wanted to take advantage of the opportunity to 'cut curricular corners' and to find some more time for mathematics and English outside the dedicated literacy and numeracy 'hours';

4. a neo-elementary curriculum: which gave continuity with their pre-1998 curriculum in the case of some schools and was a conscious choice by others feeling particularly pressurised by factors such as national numeracy and literacy strategies; Ofsted re-inspections; being in 'special measures'; having 'serious weaknesses'; performing less well than their 'benchmark' counterparts.

The revised primary curriculum

The framework and content of the national curriculum operative from Autumn 2000 are now clear (DfEE/QCA, 1999). In putting forward its proposals in 1999 the QCA's room for manoeuvre was strictly limited. The national literacy and numeracy strategies had pre-empted important decisions about overall priorities and also about the content of any revised orders for English and mathematics. Government initiatives in the area of ICT had further constrained QCA's 'degrees of freedom', as had the reports of working groups related to citizenship and to personal, social and health education. There was a strong sense that the QCA was being increasingly marginalised and that decisions with major curriculum implications were being taken on the advice of other bodies.

According to the Secretary of State (Blunkett, 1999) the revised national curriculum aimed to

*   ensure stability in schools by restricting changes to the national curriculum to the essential minimum (as defined by whom?);

*   develop a more explicit rationale for the school curriculum (but on a non-statutory basis);

- align the key stage 1 and 2 programmes of study in English and mathematics with the national frameworks for teaching literacy and mathematics (even though the latter have not been fully implemented or evaluated);

- increase flexibility (inconsistency?) by reducing prescription and the overall weight of the national curriculum at all key stages, particularly at key stages 1 and 2 in the recently designated 'non-core' subjects of design and technology, history, geography, art, music and physical education (thereby endangering children's entitlement to 'breadth' and 'balance' within as well as between the subjects of the national curriculum);

- maintain national standards (how defined?) in all subjects;

- strengthen the use of ICT across the curriculum (but with only limited 'training' planned to enable teachers to teach with ICT);

- establish a framework for personal, social and health education and citizenship at key stages 1 and 2 (but again on a non-statutory basis);

- ensure (how?) that the statutory framework, including the national curriculum, is manageable for schools (but how is this to be monitored and adjustments made?).

The primary curriculum post-2000 can be encapsulated in a second formula:

$$\underline{WC} = \underline{N} + \underline{R} + \underline{x}$$

(where $\underline{x} = \underline{pshe} + \underline{c} + \underline{k} + \underline{a}$)

ie. the whole curriculum($\underline{WC}$) comprises the national curriculum($\underline{N}$) plus religious education($\underline{R}$) plus components($\underline{x}$) including personal, social and health education($\underline{pshe}$), citizenship($\underline{c}$), key skills ($\underline{k}$) and other aspects ($\underline{a}$) such as enterprise education.

To continue the soccer analogy used earlier, the new whole curriculum comprises a series of 'divisions', only the first four of which are officially recognised in statute:

Premier Division
English
Mathematics
First Division
Science
Information and Communication Technology
Religious Education
Second Division
Design and Technology
History
Geography
Third Division
Art
Music
Physical Education
Nationwide Conference
Citizenship
Personal, social and health education
A modern foreign language
Non-League
Financial capability
Enterprise Education
Education for Sustainable Development

While the whole curriculum might appear broad in principle (though for reasons stated below it is unlikely to be realised in practice in many schools because of current political demands) the revised national curriculum represents, formally at least, a reduced legal entitlement curriculum. The word 'formally' is used advisedly because unless the regulations are strongly worded, reinforced and backed up by revised inspection/evaluation arrangements the flexibility celebrated and promised by the new statutory orders could be interpreted by some (many? most?) primary schools as giving them free rein to offer little more than a token attention to the 'third' and 'fourth division' subjects and to citizenship and personal, social and health education. If that were to happen on a large scale, a neo-elementary school curriculum might well become the norm. That curriculum would be ITEMS-based; ITEMS in two senses: IT, English, Mathematics and Science, and in the dictionary sense of 'a number of enumerated or listed things' or 'entries into an account'!

Even allowing for the inevitable mediation of policy at the level of the individual school and classroom, the 'degrees of freedom' accorded teachers in the medium term at least are likely to be far fewer than prior to 1988 and fewer too than those 'enjoyed' prior to the election of New Labour in 1997. The move towards the establishment of a reduced legal entitlement curriculum or a neo-elementary curriculum is likely to be exacerbated by other current features of the educational scene, in particular:

- the relentless attention paid by central and local government to measurable targets in English (except for listening and speaking) and mathematics – with 2002 very much in mind (and the possibility of similar, but more 'challenging', targets for 2007?);

- the increasing preoccupation of Ofsted inspections (both 'full' and 'short') with the core subjects and the scant (even token) attention paid to evaluating and reporting on the non-core subjects (Ofsted, 1999)

- the publication of school performance tables, based on test data (not teacher assessment data) in the same three core subjects;

- the increasing assessment load carried by primary pupils and teachers, especially in schools using the so-called ' optional' tests (Richards, 1999b);

- the understandable concern of primary schools in special measures or those considered to have serious weaknesses to escape that categorisation by, playing, in part at least, Ofsted's and the government's game in setting measurable targets in the tested subjects and in concentrating their efforts to meet them;

- the concern of schools (some? many? most?) to compare favourably with their so-called but inaccurately-termed 'benchmark' schools – benchmarked in relation to performance data on the same tested subjects.

The combination of the pressures exerted by these feature renders utopian the broad whole curriculum in theory available to schools from Autumn 2000 onwards.

Very significantly another feature (performance management) has been added from Autumn 2000 – one with overtones of the Victorian past (Richards, 1999a) even though cast in the garb of the 'modernisation' of the teaching profession: payment by performance. The 1999 green paper teachers: meeting the challenge of change (why no capital letters? a sign of illiteracy in government circles?) presaged the introduction of a system of performance management intended to:

- involve classroom observation and other objective evidence of performance;

- take pupil progress into account;

- result in the setting of individual targets for each teacher, at least one of which should be directly linked to the school's pupil performance targets.' (my italics) (DfEE, 1999)

How is performance, progress and target-meeting to be assessed under this 'modernised' dispensation? Largely in terms of pupils' test scores in the same three core subjects. The government claims that its performance-management framework (DfEE, 2000) is not simply a modern form of payment by results since criteria other than pupil performance will also apply in determining teachers' pay. But in the nineteenth century, although another criterion (pupil attendance) was also invoked, the criterion of meeting the standard as tested by annual examination took precedence and the effects, at least judged by critics such as Arnold (1908), were catastrophic. There is a very real danger of history repeating itself – not exactly, of course, but with similar consequences to those which befell the ill-fated policy of the latter half of the nineteenth century.

The primary curriculum in the longer term

But 'whither the primary curriculum' in the longer term once the targets have been met (as they will be), once the current moral panic over standards in the 'basics' has subsided, once performance management has been largely subverted and once our position in the international league tables for literacy and mathematics (though probably not science) has improved ? The QCA's plans for ongoing monitoring and investigation of selected issues (such as the place of modern languages in primary education) will not be sufficient to provide the radical review that is required.

There needs to be a genuine national debate over the future form and content of the school curriculum. To be thorough and to involve all 'stakeholders' it needs to take place over a number of years (in contrast to the hurried partial consultations of recent years), drawing on both independent and government-sponsored evaluations of the strategies and initiatives conducted in different parts of the UK since 1988. It needs to be unconstrained by current structures, strategies and policies, and it needs to focus on what constitutes an educated person and on the kind of education the young should experience and contribute to (rather than merely 'be taught') in the early part of the twenty-first century. This genuinely 'great' debate should involve not just those employed in the education service but also parents, governors, local and national politicians, the wider community and, particularly, the young themselves. Such a long-term project on a time-scale not determined by the date of general elections and resulting in a new truly national curriculum, published in 2010 or thereabouts and implemented some years later after properly funded and targeted professional development, would provide a millennial focus for the nation's aspirations for its children, its most precious long-term asset.

It needs to focus on two related key questions:

'How can education, especially the school system and the school curriculum, be reshaped to operate effectively in the new landscape?

How can it continue to provide the basic outcomes which every student needs, while also equipping and motivating them for challenges which we have not yet been able to imagine?' (Bentley, 2000)

It needs to respond to the four challenges laid down in All Our Futures (National Advisory Committee on Creative and Cultural Education 1999):

'Economic

To develop in young people the skills, knowledge and personal qualities they need for a world where work is undergoing rapid and long-term change.

Technological

To enable young people to make their way with confidence in a world that is being shaped by technologies which are evolving more quickly than at any time in history.

Social

To provide forms of education that enable young people to engage positively and confidently with far-reaching processes of social and cultural change.

Personal

To develop the unique capacities of all young people, and to provide a basis on which they can each build lives that are purposeful and fulfilling.'

Such a review might raise and seek a consensus on a number of questions related to the primary curriculum, such as:

The nature and extent of legal prescription

- Should a primary curriculum be legally prescribed at all ?

- If so at what level – local? regional? country? UK? European Union? United Nations?

- What are the components that should be legally prescribed – aims and purposes? content? assessment? organisation? teaching methodology?

- Should different components be prescribed at different levels?

- Should a total primary curriculum be prescribed or should there be elements of discretion; if the latter at what levels?

- Should the notions of 'stages' or 'levels' be retained?

The rationale for the curriculum

- What should be the core aims and values a primary curriculum is attempting to promote?

- What personal qualities, skills, intelligences, understandings and knowledge should primary-aged children develop as a result of engagement with such a curriculum?

- How far should a primary curriculum attend to such issues as

  - economic and work-place needs in the context of change, globalisation, Internet access and uncertainty;

  - individual development, freedom and fulfilment;

  - personal and collective morality;

  - social justice, social inclusion and social cohesion;

  - culture, broadly and pluralistically conceived;

  - citizenship in a democratic society.

The content of the curriculum

- How should the curriculum be conceptualised: in terms of skill domains? subjects? broad areas? areas of learning? dimensions? modules? topics? or a combination of these?

- What should be the place of key skills such as creative thinking, enquiry, information-processing, question posing, problem solving and improvement of own learning ?

- Should a primary curriculum provide more or less than whatever is the current range of core and other subjects?

- If less, which should be omitted and when?

- If more, which should be included -a modern foreign language, drama, philosophy, social psychology, anthropology?

- Should a primary curriculum make provision for cross-curricular themes and if so, which and when? Should new candidates be considered, eg media education, European studies?

- Should the curriculum give explicit attention to teaching children transferable metacognitive skills? What are these? How can they be fostered?

- How far can, or should, the content be continually revised in the light of developments in ICT?

Assessment in the curriculum

- Should all elements of a primary curriculum be assessed or only a 'core'. If a 'core',of what should it comprise?

- Who should be involved in that assessment? – government (local, national or regional?), teachers? carers? the children themselves?

- What forms should that assessment take?

- When should those forms be used?

- What should assessment data be used for?

- How should assessment data be reported ?

There are doubtless many more questions and issues that might be raised – particularly by the young themselves!

References

Alexander R, Willcock J and Nelson N, (1995) 'Change and Continuity' in Alexander R Versions of Primary Education, London: Routledge

Arnold M (1908) Reports on Elementary Schools 1852-1882, London: His Majesty's Stationery Office

Bentley T (2000) 'Learning for a creative age' in Education Futures, London: RSA/ Design Council

Blunkett D (1999) The review of the national curriculum in England. The Secretary of State's Proposals, London: Qualifications and Curriculum Authority

Broadfoot P et al (2000) Promoting Quality in Learning: Does England have the answer? London: Cassell

Campbell R, (1997) Standards of Literacy and Numeracy in Primary Schools: a real or manufactured crisis? Occasional paper, CREPE, University of Warwick

Campbell R and Neil S, (1994a) Primary Teachers at Work, London: Routledge

Campbell R and Neil S, (1994b) Curriculum Reform at Key Stage 1: teacher commitment and policy failure, London: Longman

Dann R and Simco N (2000) 'Teachers in charge: a speculative vision of the future of primary education' Education 3-13 28:1

Davis A (1999) The Limits of Educational Assessment Oxford: Blackwell

Dearing R, (1993) The National Curriculum and Assessment: final report London: School Curriculum and Assessment Authority

Department of Education and Science (DES), (1988) National Curriculum Task Group on Assessment and Testing: A Report London:Department of Education and Science

Department for Education and Employment (DfEE), (1997a) Excellence in Schools London: Her Majesty's Stationery Office

Department for Education and Employment (DfEE), (1997b) The Implementation of the National Literacy Strategy London: Department for Education and Employment

Department for Education and Employment (DfEE) (1999) Teachers meeting the challenge of change, London: Her Majesty's Stationery Office

Department for Education and Employment (DfEE) (2000) Performance Management in Schools, London: Department for Education and Employment

Department for Education and Employment (DfEE) and Qualifications and Curriculum Authority (QCA) (1999) The National Curriculum: Handbook for primary teachers in England, London: Her Majesty's Stationery Office

Galton M, (1998) Reliving the ORACLE experience: back to basics or back to the future? Occasional paper, CREPE, University of Warwick

Galton M et al (1999) Inside the Primary Classroom: 20 years on, London: Routledge

Galton M and Fogelman K, (1997) The Use of Discretionary Time in the Primary School, Final report of research commissioned by the National Union of Teachers, University of Leicester School of Education

Galton M and Morris P, (1998), 'The real lessons from the Pacific Rim' Education 3-13 26:2

National Advisory Committee on Creative and Cultural Education (1999) All Our Futures: Creativity, Culture and Education, London: Department for Education and Employment

Office for Standards in Education (Ofsted) (1999) Handbook for Inspecting Primary and Nursery Schools London: Her Majesty's Stationery Office

Plewis I and Veltman M, (1996) 'Where does all the time go?: changes in pupils' experience in Year 2 classrooms'; in Hughes M (ed) Teaching and Learning in Changing Times Oxford:Blackwell

Pollard A et al, (1994) Changing English Primary Schools? London: Cassell

Richards C, (1997a), 'Enrichment as entitlement' in Developing the Primary School Curriculum: the next steps London: School Curriculum and Assessment Authority

Richards C, (1997b), 'The primary curriculum 1988-2008' British Journal of Curriculum and Assessment 7:3

Richards C (1999) The Primary Curriculum: past, present and future ASPE Paper 8, Stoke-on-Trent, Trentham Books

Richards C (1999) 'Testing times' The Teacher December

THROUGH A GLASS DARKLY:
assessing the future?

Colin Conner

Since the introduction of the national curriculum in 1988, it is probably fair to say that the issue that has created the greatest tension for primary schools has been assessment. The continual changing of curriculum expectations and assessment requirements, and recent demands for careful quantitative analysis of assessment results to inform decision making has left many schools uncertain about exactly what is expected of them. This trend has been exacerbated by requirements to set appropriate achievement targets, especially for literacy and numeracy, at the level of the school, the class and for each individual. The effectiveness of this process is dependent on systems of assessment and analysis being in place and on the skills of teachers in their use. But with all the changes that have taken place, is there anything that we have learned from our experience of applying assessment in schools? This chapter explores assessment from the perspective of the past and the present and suggests ways in which assessment might change in the future. It is argued that our effort in the future should be aimed at developing our skills of assessment for learning rather than the current obsession with the assessment of learning. It is also suggested that technology might be an important means by which teachers can make the process more manageable.

Introduction

In a recent discussion with a group of primary and secondary teachers I invited them to reflect on the main issues that they were coping with as far as assessment is concerned. The main things that came out from this discussion were as follows:

- an increasing emphasis on accountability

- an increasing focus on standards and progress

- the increasing importance of data collection and analysis

- comparisons within and beyond school through benchmarking, PANDA reports and the Autumn Package

- an analysis of assessments and projecting children's achievements both forwards and backwards. (That is, reflecting on what analysis tells you about children's achievements and what the future implications should/might be)

- an emphasis on target setting at the level of the individual, the class, the subject and the school

- the analysis of children's responses to tests to provide useful diagnostic information for teachers.

- the dominance of assessment and especially summative assessment

Whilst I think most teachers would accept all of the above and agree that our curriculum is currently dominated by summative assessment, what of the future? In this article I propose to offer some reflections on the past with a view to identifying opportunities that might be presented for the immediate and longer term future.

The immediate past

I will live in the past, the present and the future.
I will strive to learn from the lessons of all three.
(Charles Dickens – A Christmas Carol)

It seems a considerable time since the publication of the report of the Task Group on Assessment and Testing (DES, 1988), which attempted to construct a model upon which the assessment of the national curriculum was to be based. To many, the proposals it contained were far too complex, whilst others were impressed by the group's creative attempt at satisfying the external pressure for an assessment system that provided summative, formative, and diagnostic evidence as well as evidence that could be used to judge the effectiveness of the education system. One of the leading assessment experts of the time, the late Desmond Nuttall (1987), argued categorically that there wasn't an assessment system in existence anywhere in the world that could use the same information for such a diverse range of purposes. As a result, different purposes dominated and the TGAT proposals that teachers' assessments should carry the same weight as formal, externally monitored assessments quickly lost ground. We now have an assessment system where SATs dominate and with the introduction of league tables at key stage 2, these tests have assumed 'high stakes' status. They influence what is taught and narrow the curriculum experience of children. As a year 6 teacher recently argued,

> Six years ago, when key stage 2 tests were first introduced, the teacher put children in for the test to see where they were at. Now we start the year teaching to the tests. We are not developing the whole child, English, maths and science are the priorities, at the expense of nearly all other parts of the curriculum. (Slaven, 1999: 14)

This narrowing of the curriculum has not been helped by the imposition of numeracy and literacy strategies as part of the drive to improve standards.

For nearly 20 years there has been a steady warning that educational standards in the United Kingdom are declining. For example in 1977, the DES consultative document, Education in Schools, commented that 'children's standards of performance in their school work is said to have declined. The curriculum pays too little attention to the basic skills of reading, writing and arithmetic and is overloaded with fringe subjects.'

But are standards falling? A review of literacy and numeracy standards between 1948 and 1994 by Brooks et al. (1995: 3) for the National Commission on Education concluded that

> The major feature of the results throughout the UK is their great stability over time; most comparisons reveal no change, a few show a rise, even fewer show a fall... and there is certainly no warrant for doom-laden pronouncements of inexorable decline.

Comparisons with other countries present a different picture, however, and suggest that England's performance relative to other countries has been falling. (Keys et al., 1996).

Pring (1992) reminds us that what goes up or down is not the standard, but the performance of pupils against the standard, so that declining standards means that performance is not coming up to the standard to the extent that it once did, or that performance is coming up to a standard that is now different. He suggests that standards have 'neither gone up nor down, they have simply changed'. This is the case to some extent with the international comparisons where it is difficult to establish a set of assessments that equate to the curriculum that is taught in all of the participating countries and it is exactly what has happened with the national curriculum. Standards and expectations have changed so often since its introduction, it is difficult to have confidence in the assessments themselves despite the fact that the government has invested heavily in their comparative credibility. This is an issue that has been stressed by Tymms (1999: 13) who suggests that we do not have a satisfactory way of measuring standards from year to year. He argues that

> The root of the problem is that statutory tests are being asked to do too many things. They are there to diagnose individual pupil difficulties, to check curriculum coverage, to give information to parents, to check on teachers and to assess value added as well as monitoring standards over time... Psychometricians have long understood the difficulties of checking standards over time − the language of a culture changes over the years, attitudes to testing change, the curriculum changes, technology intervenes and so on.

The limitations of the assessment processes that are currently being used have also been commented upon by Robinson (1997: 2) in his evaluation of standards of literacy and numeracy and their relationship to economic performance:

> Given that the results of the Standard Assessment tasks have only been available nationally for 11 year olds since 1995, it might be a brave policy maker who would want to set policy around National Targets for attainment at age 11 using the SAT results. Yet the policy making agenda of the new Labour Government is based precisely around the use of SATs... Before the government sets ambitious targets for attainment in literacy and numeracy at age 11 using the SATs results as a benchmark, it must be satisfied that they can really be relied upon.

Given these concerns where should schools be diverting their effort in the attempt to raise standards? A number of writers and researchers argue that our effort should be aimed at developing our skills of assessment for learning rather than the current obsession with assessment of learning. James (1998: 171) reinforces this when she suggests:

> Since the purpose of schools is the education of children, assessments have little value unless they contribute to that purpose. They should help students to learn better and, in so doing, raise their achievements and contribute to school improvement. Assessment results alone cannot do this because, as the saying goes, you cannot fatten the pig simply by weighing it. Something has to be done with the assessment data. Assessment of learning is therefore insufficient for educational purposes; assessment for learning is necessary.

Improving assessment in the immediate future

This idea that we should focus attention on assessment for learning, that assessment can be built into teaching to enhance learning, is at the heart of the concept of formative assessment. It has been the subject of a variety of recent research projects (Torrance and Pryor, 1998; Tunstall and Gipps, 1996). The most recent research on the topic, however, has been undertaken by Black and Wiliam (1998) and their findings suggest that one way to improve assessment and at the same time improve standards is to concentrate on developing our practice of formative assessment.

> ...standards are raised only by changes that are put into direct effect by teachers and pupils in classrooms...Our education system has been subjected to many far reaching initiatives which, whilst taken in relation to concerns about existing practice, have been based on little evidence about their potential to meet these concerns. In our study...there can be seen, for once, firm evidence that indicates a clear direction for change which could improve standards of learning. (Black and Wiliam, 1998: 19)

Black and Wiliam define formative assessment in terms of all the activities undertaken by teachers and/or by children, which provide information which can be used as feedback to modify teaching and learning; '...assessment becomes 'formative assessment' when the evidence is actually used to adapt the teaching work to meet learning needs' (p.2).

The work of Sadler was a significant influence on their thinking. Sadler (1989) argued that formative assessment should be concerned with how judgements about the quality of a child's response can be used by the teacher to shape and improve their understanding. As a result,

> Where anyone is trying to learn, feedback about their efforts has three elements – the desired goal, the evidence about their present position, and some understanding of a way to close the gap between the two (Sadler, 1989). All three must to a degree be understood by anyone before they can take action to improve their learning. New understanding cannot be forced in. It has to be incorporated with existing ideas, so changing them if necessary, by thoughtful actions taken by the learner. (Black and Wiliam, 1998: 10)

To illustrate the significance of formative assessment for the improvement of learning, Black and Wiliam reviewed over 580 articles worldwide. In one Portuguese study reported by Fontana and Fernandes (1994), 25 teachers undertook an in-service course to study methods for teaching pupils to assess themselves. During the 20 week part-time course, the teachers put the ideas into practice with children aged between 8 and 14. These children were given a test before the project started and at the end of the project so that gains could be measured. The same tests were also taken by a control group. The self-assessment group's gains were twice that of the control group. In the self-assessment group, the focus was on regular self-assessment often on a daily basis. It involved teaching students to understand both the learning objectives for each lesson and the assessment criteria, giving them an opportunity to select learning tasks and using tasks that allowed them scope to assess their own learning outcomes.

The implication of this is that self-assessment by pupils is essential. As has been demonstrated, however (Tunstall and Gipps, 1996), practice in primary schools tends not to give the involvement of the learner the credence it deserves. In their study of formative assessment and feedback in primary classrooms, a significant proportion of assessments emphasised either reward/approval or punishment/ disapproval. Some of the most effective forms of feedback were described as 'specifying attainment and specifying improvement', but even here the feedback is directed from the teacher to the child, with the teacher telling the child what is good and what else can be done to improve. What needs to be developed according to Stobart and Gipps (1997) is an emphasis in feedback which 'constructs achievement' and 'constructs the way forward'. In each of these categories, it is more of a conversation and discussion with the learner with the aim being to identify future possibilities. With this kind of feedback, teachers involve the learner in explaining and developing their understanding of the quality of their work using the child's own work. Strategies are identified that could be adopted to develop the work and the child is encouraged in the constructive assessment of their own work, to 'close the gap' between what they are able to do now and what they are capable of in the future.

Perrenoud (1998: 86-7) argues that feedback may well have an effect on children's learning because it affects their thinking about themselves as learners. However, it will only have an effect if the learner knows what to do with the information provided by a teacher and, more importantly, wants to do anything with it. He suggests that

> This intention can only be effective if a window can be found into the cognitive system of the learner. There is no point sending him or her messages if they are treated as noise or redundancy, and not intelligible or pertinent information likely to help him understand, remember, assimilate knowledge or develop skills. Thus we must concede that some of the messages which the teacher conceives as feedback do not in fact play this role for the pupil, because their form, their tone, their content (verbal and non-verbal), the moment chosen, the point reached in the work and the interactive situation in which they occur do not allow the pupils to understand them 'to do something' with them.

The implications of the ideas of Black and Wiliam have been explored by the Assessment Reform Group, a collaboration between some of the leading assessment researchers in the UK. In a pamphlet published in 1999 and entitled 'Assessment for Learning: Beyond the Black Box', they argue that the Black and Wiliam study suggests that improving learning through assessment depends on five deceptively simple key factors:

- the provision of effective feedback to pupils

- the active involvement of pupils in their own learning

- adjusting teaching to take account of the results of assessments

- a recognition of the profound influence assessment has on the motivation and self-esteem of pupils, both of which are crucial influences on learning

- the need for pupils to be able to assess themselves and understand how to improve

As was suggested earlier, and emphasised in the above comments, for assessment to be formative, feedback information has to be used by the learner. As a result it needs to

- be based on clear learning intentions and success criteria

- take account of the child's own self-evaluation

- highlight where success has occurred and where improvements could take place

- be in a form that is accessible and understandable to the learner

- have time allocated for it to take place and for the children to read it/and/or discuss it with their teacher

- have strategies suggested for improvement which are clearly focused and based on the feedback

Having identified ways in which assessment might be improved in the immediate future, what of the longer term?

Improving Assessment in the longer term

One of the major difficulties any primary teacher faces in attempting to improve the quality and quantity of feedback to learners when it is really needed is the sheer number of children she has to deal with. There are any number of occasions in a busy primary classroom when learning is taking place and the teacher is not there to reinforce or confirm it. It is simply not possible to be in the right place at the right time for all learning. It is also the case that what learners most often need is immediate feedback to sustain motivation and interest. This is where in the future, technology might offer support to the hard pressed teacher. Michael Barber, Head of the Standards and Effectiveness unit at the DfEE, has argued that investment should be 'directed into making use of information technology to assist with assessment'. (Barber, 1996: 202). Similarly, Tom Bentley (1998), from the independent think-tank Demos, has suggested that technology ought to provide us with the opportunity to develop an on-going record of an individual's personal achievements, not only whilst in school, but throughout their working life. As Thomson (1996) suggests,

It is something of a cliché to say that we are truly on the threshold of a revolution which will affect the way we all learn. It remains true however that, not since the invention of the 'modern' printing press over 500 years ago, has anything happened to rival the dramatic development in new communication technologies and their potential to influence positively the way we all learn. If developed and used properly, it could also significantly influence the way we assess.

As an illustration of how this is already happening, QCA (1999) has provided details of every standard assessment task that has been used so far at key stages 1, 2 and 3 on a CD-ROM. In future, schools can create their own assessments from past SATs to inform them of their children's progress when they think it would be helpful. It is also proposed that assessments can be undertaken on-line from 2003. Michael Barber (1996: 134-5) illustrates the use of ICT in a Birmingham primary school:

The school commissioned an IT package to provide an assessment data base which could be used in a variety of ways. Assessment data is used, for example, to identify and provide for differentiated groups of pupils. Teachers log assessment data from the core subjects every term. They use the information to select teaching groups for different purposes...Teachers can direct progress and re-deploy resources in the most sensible way...The formal recording of progress at regular intervals allows the class teacher and the Special Needs Co-ordinator to see how best to arrange the support for individuals and groups of children as well as giving a more finely tuned indication of progress than the National Curriculum levels alone.'

This broader conception of assessment and the associated use of technology is further illustrated in a Boston elementary school. All teachers have their own hand held computer. As they interact with individuals during the day and see 'significant' examples of progress for individuals, this is noted on the computer. Not everything is noted, only evidence of significant gains for individual children. At the end of the day the information is downloaded by the school secretary on to the page for each child. At the end of the week the teachers take home their classes' details. These are used for reflection and planning for the following week. As a result, the teachers have found the curriculum becoming more individualised. Meetings with parents have also improved because of the quality of the data that has been collected which is used as a basis for discussions about progress. No significant illustrations of progress are lost in this process. This is just one example of how formative assessments can be collected and used with the aid of technology.

Another example comes from University of California in Los Angeles (UCLA). For over 30 years, the UCLA Centre for the Study of Evaluation has been at the forefront of efforts to develop ways in which assessment and reporting systems may be supported by technology. The Centre for Research on Evaluation, Standards and Student Testing, CRESST for short, argues that there are three qualities that are essential to the productive use of assessment namely validity, fairness and credibility. As can be seen in the CRESST model (Land, 1997), collectively these ensure that assessment information is utilised. The notion of utility is fundamental to the previous discussion about formative assessment. 'Is the information useful and usable?'

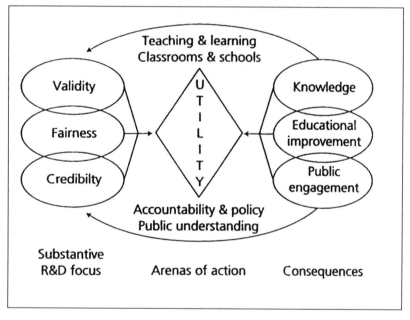

Figure 1: CRESST Conceptual model (Land, 1997)

At CRESST, they are in the process of developing computer-based assessment systems which require children to solve problems during and at the end of units of work. Rather than just repeat what has already been learned, the children have to select from a range of data what they believe is needed to solve the problem. The World Wide Web can be an important part of this information base. Not only does the printout of the children's solution to each of these problems tell the teacher about each child's progress in comparison with a standard, and their peers, it also provides information about the pathways to their solution. In other words, both summative and formative information is produced. This can be used by the teacher for further development with individuals and groups and as an evaluation of the effectiveness of teaching, as well as to produce standardised information for accountability purposes. With the proposed improvements to technology in schools in the UK and increased teacher skills following the advent of targeted training in this area, the future does indeed look promising. We shall have to wait and see! Certainly the two examples described here give us hope, if only the technology, resources and appropriate training are made available. Also, given the importance of the learners in the process, Galton *et al.* (1999: 170) remind us that

> ...we need to ensure that all children know how to exploit the technology to solve their problems. In other words, as children's horizons expand, so does the need for a broad curriculum consisting of cognitively challenging tasks and appropriately sophisticated and valid forms of assessment, whose reliability would increase as teachers gained more experience, confidence and faith in its value. This will not be achieved, however, as long as we have such 'high stakes' assessment – as long as teachers feel the aim of assessment is to move their schools up the league table, rather than to support children's learning.

References

Assessment Reform Group (1999) Assessment for Learning: Beyond the Black Box, Cambridge, University of Cambridge School of Education

Barber, M. (1996) The Learning Game. Arguments for an Education Revolution, London, Victor Gollancz

Bentley, T. (1998) Learning beyond the Classroom. Education for a changing world, London, Routledge

Black, P. and Wiliam, D. (1998) Inside the Black Box: Raising Standards through Classroom Assessment, London: Kings College School of Education

Brooks, G., Foxman, D. and Gorman, T. (1995) Standards in Literacy and Numeracy 1948-94, National Commission on Education Briefing, new series, Slough: NFER

DES (1977) Education in Schools, London: HMSO

DES (1988) Task Group on Assessment and Testing: A Report, London: HMSO

Galton, M., Hargreaves, L.,Comber, C.,Wall, D. and Pell, A. (1999) Inside the Primary Classroom 20 Years On, London: Routledge

Fontana, D. and Fernandes, M. (1994) 'Improvements in mathematics performance as a consequence of self-assessment in Portuguese primary school children', British Journal of Educational psychology, 64, 407-417

James, M. (1998) Using Assessment for School Improvement, London: Heinemann

Keys,W., Harris, S. and Fernandes, C. (1996) Third International Mathematics and Science Study: First Report: Part 1, Slough: NFER

Nuttall, D. (1987) 'The validity of assessments', European Journal of Psychology of Education, II: 2

Perrenoud, P. (1998) 'From Formative Evaluation to a Controlled Regulation of Learning Processes. Toward a wider conceptual field', Assessment in Education, 5:1

Pring, R. (1992) 'Standards and Quality in Education', British Journal of Educational Studies, 1

QCA (1999) Key Stage 1,2 and3 test compendium CD, London, QCA and Double-struck Ltd. Reference QCA/99/520

Robinson, P. (1997) Literacy, Numeracy and Economic Performance, London: Centre for Economic Performance

Sadler, D.R. (1989) 'Formative assessment and the design of instructional systems', Instructional Science, 18

Slaven, S. (1999) 'Primary testing is too much too soon', Times Educational Supplement, 9-4-99.

Stobart, G.and Gipps, C. (1997) Assessment: A teachers' guide to the issues, London: Hodder and Stoughton

Thomson, P. (1996) 'Hi, tech future', in For Life. A vision for learning in the 21st century, London, Royal Society of Arts

Torrance, H. and Pryor, J. (1998) Investigating Formative Assessment. Teaching, Learning and Assessment in the Classroom, Buckingham: Open University Press

Tunstall, P and Gipps, G. (1996) 'How does your teacher help you make your work better? Children's understanding of formative assessment', The Curriculum Journal,7: 2

Tymms, P. (1999) 'Hitting a moving target', Association for the Study of Primary Education Newsletter, Spring

ASSESSING SCHOOLS:
quantity is no substitute
for quality
Norman Thomas

HMI: general and specialist roles

Before the creation of Ofsted, HM Inspectorate of Schools was concerned with schools and further education, including some aspects of higher education. Its members had, between them, experience of working in institutions across that range. The great majority of HMI in England lived and mainly worked within one of seven geographically-defined Divisions – reduced from ten as motorways extended and transport became easier. Each field HMI had a generalist function that required her or him to get to know a group of institutions – schools in my case – and the authorities responsible for them, typically the LEAs, and especially the CEOs, administrators, local advisers and inspectors. Formal inspections leading to an issued report were almost invariably arranged, and the report written, by the general inspector for the institution, who had seen examples of teaching during previous visits and knew a fair amount about the local circumstances. The work in each Division was overseen by one of its members, the Divisional Inspector. HMI were usually moved from one Division to another at about seven-year intervals, though special circumstances might dictate other-wise. Movement was important so as to reduce the risk of local prejudice.

Each general inspector had a specialism. It may have been in a phase of education, for example nursery and infant schools or teacher training, or a subject of the curriculum, or an aspect of education, for

57

example the education of the deaf. The specialist work, overseen nationally by a specialist Staff Inspector, required the HMI to operate over a wider geographical area than that covered by the general assignment, usually across a Division but in some cases, for example for the deaf or in the conduct of a national survey, across England.

HMI: training and cross-checking

Every post-1944 entrant went through a probationary period, at first of two years but later reduced to one year. The Divisional Inspector, the relevant specialist Staff Inspector and the local HMI mentor to whom the newcomer was attached, arranged a programme that ensured his or her increasing independence of operation, but also required the probationer, under supervision, to observe aspects of education with which he or she was not familiar: schools with different age groups of pupils or in different contexts, further education institutes, youth clubs and other provision that was outside the HMI's former experience. The purpose was to enable the probationer to understand better the broad educational context within which his or her main work would be done, to demonstrate the range of practices being adopted and to warn against glib assumptions that what the new HMI had previously done was the answer for every occasion. Each HMI concerned with the inspection of schools had a folder containing guidance on the factors to be taken into account when inspecting schools of different kinds.

Every visit, during the probationary period and afterwards, led to a written account of the work observed, its effectiveness and the comments made to those seen. The notes were kept by the general inspector in a file devoted to that institution so that they would inform future visits, whether made by this or a future general inspector or by a specialist HMI called in for a particular purpose.

The HMI within a Division met as a group every year or two for a couple of days and discussed, under pre-arranged themes, the issues of current interest. Smaller groups, for example the Divisional Primary Committee, also met regularly, but more often, to consider relevant aspects of the work. The specialists, of whatever kind, were formed into national committees under the chairmanship of the appropriate Staff Inspector to share views and experiences on matters and trends that were, or were thought ought to be, of national interest.

Either through personal initiative, or through discussion at the Divisional or national committees, focused surveys were arranged to illuminate practice in an identified aspect of education: the teaching of English in the 'top' years (year 6 in today's terminology) of primary schools in Middlewich; or the effects of 'open-plan' school design; or, in the 1970s, the primary education provided across England for selected age groups.

When formal (sometimes misleadingly called 'full') inspections or surveys were carried out, for example for national primary surveys, care was taken to arrange that the teams of inspectors were continually shuffled so that each member had to test his or her view against those of other HMI ordinarily working in different parts of the country. Equally, views were tested and updated through attendance at specialist courses organised by HMI mainly for teachers, but which brought together leading individuals from inside and outside the Inspectorate. Members of an inspection team stayed in a local hotel and were joined by the local, general/reporting inspector, so that a good deal of discussion went on each evening during the period of an inspection, and was conducted more formally at the 'Thursday evening' meeting when conclusions were drawn in readiness for presentation to the headteacher and to other members of staff the following morning. The meeting with the governors usually took place after the reporting inspector had written the first draft of the report.

The purposes of inspection

The purposes of visits, whether leading to a published report or not, were to find out what was being done, to judge its effectiveness, and, as one went, to promote and support increased effectiveness. Effectiveness had, crudely, two aspects: (a) was the school achieving what it set out to do; (b) was what it intended sufficient? Every school that I have visited has wanted its pupils to learn how to read and write.

As an example of the first aspect, to what extent were the children (all, most, some) acquiring these skills? And of the second, to what extent were they

- being taught to become increasingly independent learners:

- seeking out information for themselves through books, through direct observation and experimentation;

- learning to use the library and various tools and media;

- engaging in and profiting from discussion among themselves and with the teacher;

- recording, in words and a range of media, what they had learnt and felt?

Not all schools are so clear in this second set of intentions. If there was a serious deficiency then the need for remediation had to be made plain to the individuals concerned: the teacher(s), the head-teacher, the adviser, the CEO or whoever; but that was not the goal of the inspection. HMI did not set out to discover weakness, but was required to alert those responsible for dealing with it when found. Equally, it was important to make sure that especially effective practice was known. When I was a teacher, it was an HMI who put me in touch with another teacher who was able to show me what he was doing, with considerable success, in teaching children who had substantial difficulties in learning to read. The HMI programme of short courses for teachers and the series of pamphlets were more formal ways of doing the same thing.

Formal inspections and surveys

Until the mid-1970s, individual HMI had a very considerable personal independence in the organisation of their programmes of work. They were, however, called into formal inspection teams, most arranged at a Divisional level; their specialist advice was sought by other HMI; and they welcomed formal membership of the national specialist teams, which also affected their work patterns. From the mid-1970s more and more exercises were arranged nationally. The national primary school and secondary school surveys were prominent examples. They were based on samples of schools. The samples were large by most research standards, of over 500 schools in the case of the national primary school survey, but did not encompass all maintained schools, as does a full cycle of Ofsted inspections. However, HMI did, in the early 1950s, set out to conduct a formal, reporting inspection on every maintained school and largely carried the intention through. Additionally, in the mid-1960s, HMI provided the Plowden Committee with assessments of 19,988 English primary schools of the 20,664 then in existence, most based on routine 'informal' visits. Formal inspections were conducted according to a common framework covering the context in which the school operated, its membership – staff and pupils – organisation, curriculum, building and resources; but there was no National Curriculum and HMI published no specific criteria by which a school would be judged. In the case of the surveys, there were itemised schedules against which HMI made their returns and that allowed a more detailed statistical analysis to be made of the information and assessments recorded. Even so, care was taken to avoid an over-precise interpretation: in the national primary survey, based on over a million items of information, a typical statement is, 'Nine out of ten 11-year-old classes were taught to carry out calculations involving the four rules of number to two decimal places or more.'

By contrast, Ofsted's contracted inspections are all formal and of all maintained schools (though the cycle is crumbling in a way that reminds me of the later 1950s) and they are conducted with the terms of the National Curriculum in mind – which, it needs to be noticed, are already becoming less precise with the passage of time. The schools also know a good deal about the criteria that are to be used during the inspections, since they are set out in the published documents. But it is equally important to understand that judgements based on those criteria may well be and often are dependent on the experience, knowledge and predilections of the person applying them. The fact that there is an enormous database, easily tapped and arranged, does not mean that the information extracted is more (or less) reliable than that which came up through the discussions of groups of HMI or the more structured surveys that they carried out. The quality of the basic information is more important than its volume. As an astute ILEA inspector used to say about overhead projectors, 'If you put a little 'rubbish' on the film, you get big 'rubbish' up on the screen.'

Achieving and sustaining quality of assessment

There are two reasons to be cautious about the quality of the assessments being made, and a third to warn that their quality may decrease with time, given the continuation of the present Ofsted pattern. The first concerns the selection and training of new inspectors. The large numbers of people recruited make it impossible to know as much about the individuals chosen as was the case in pre-Ofsted days. Even then, mistakes were sometimes made and the probationary period was not lightly treated. A careful check was kept on the HMI's performance by the Divisional Inspector, the relevant Staff Inspector and, during the probationary period, by the appointed mentor. The present checks are far less comprehensive. The training was, as has been described above, much more extensive than the few days now provided. It was necessary to learn not only the procedures for inspection and reporting and to practise them under supervision for a year or more, but also to experience a far wider range of circumstances, within one's own specialism and beyond it. In this way, the important personal experience that was brought into the Inspectorate was extended and contextualised. Writing from my own experience, I can hardly describe how vital I found that process to be when making the range of judgements required of me.

The second concerns the interchange of views, both during inspections and outside them, between the inspectors. The need to express, defend and sometimes to change a view in the light of new evidence was an important and continuing aid to perception and interpretation when inspecting. The present bidding groups of inspectors are too small, and often too parochial, to allow the breadth of interchange that I found invaluable. LEA groups can be better placed in that sense than private groups. If my informants are right, the funding of inspections has been so reduced that it is hardly possible – my informants say not possible – for an inspection team to be accommodated in a single hotel and so have the opportunity to test out and exchange views and knowledge at the end of each day's inspection, as was the custom even when Ofsted began its first cycle of inspections.

The third comes with the inescapable passage of time. Although many new inspectors had to be trained and recruited at the beginning of Ofsted's work, it was also possible to draw on people with long experience as inspectors, either HMI or local authority or both. Their numbers are reducing and will go on reducing. Many of the new inspectors have not had and will not have the advantage of making unannounced visits to many schools, as was the custom of HMI.

It has always been thought by some that the main advantage of a formal, reporting inspection is the change carried out by the institution between the notice being served and the actual visitation. There is probably something in that, but I had more confidence that I was learning about the everyday work of schools from what I saw and heard during unannounced visits, which occupied the bulk of my time as a field HMI. The question, and it goes to the heart of HMI/Ofsted comparison, is whether the main purpose is to report on the day-to-day operation of the system as it is, or to expose weakness, or, even, to promote change. (Note: the question I raise is about balance and priority; all three aspects must be present.)

The collation of results
There is no doubt that Ofsted has a far more substantial, computerised database than was available to HM Inspectorate. It is a characteristic of computer databases that those entering information have to compress it so that it fits the shape of the program. It is possible to have teachers divided into seven levels of competence, but they each go into only one and not the other six, though the various aspects of their competence may not be of a piece. To reach a judgement about schools in general, a school, or even a teacher, a degree of simplification is required. That does not, I think, make the process worthless; I was, after all, engaged in making judgements of pupils when a teacher and of schools when an HMI. But the process requires a degree of humility on the part of the assessors. That is perhaps what has been most lacking in Ofsted in recent years.

Where next?

The lengthening of the cycle of inspections is an indication that the regular, formal inspection of every school is no longer seen as an effective or economic way of improving the education system in a general sense. Mr Woodhead is already mentioning 'spot checks'. The softening of the National Curriculum will probably extend, though the pressure on primary schools to adopt the literacy and numeracy 'hours' gives rise to new measures against which schools can be judged. Even those initiatives are likely to run out of steam as their novelty wears off, though I trust that the useful elements that they contain will persist. In the longer run, the optimist in me hopes that the idea will come to dawn again that the best way of invigorating the work of schools is to encourage the teachers to use their initiative in ways that are both imaginative and rigorous. To do so, they need time, space, resources and effective, continuing training. The financial support for those is the responsibility of the government, which needs to know what to support and to have some means of satisfying itself that the funds are being spent for the purposes intended and with good effect.

The inspection of schools will continue to be necessary as part of the process of determining the effectiveness of the system and for the identification of priorities for action at local, regional and governmental levels. The organisation of inspection will depend upon the division of responsibilities for action.

My own belief is that there will be a movement towards regionalisation in the initial and continuing training of teachers and of the oversight of the school system. Local authorities and local university/training establishments may well continue, but their operations, separately and together, will be coordinated regionally. The extension of higher education to larger and larger proportions of the population seems likely to add to the pressure to make initial teacher training a wholly postgraduate process. That could well enhance the status of teaching, but to be adequate the course needs to take two-years, probably with the first year mainly in the postgraduate institution and the second mainly in schools. It should also be seen as simply the first stage in continuous training throughout the teacher's career – and to a far greater extent than now. Furthermore, the training requires far closer coordination between the trainers, the system providers and the inspection services than currently exists.

The regions will need their own inspection services and will also draw on the research done by the staff of the regional training institutions and increasingly by teachers. The government will continue to require its own independent inspection advice, but I doubt that it will wish to re-create HM Inspectorate in its former size. It is more likely to want a relatively small force, mostly operating from regional bases (but with some central staff) tapping into and influencing the work of the regional inspectorates.

Changes in the populations from which new teachers are recruited – more new teachers qualifying later in life are likely to want to work reasonably locally – as well as the broader inclination of governments, seem likely to push in the direction of regionalisation. If that is developed, then it is to be hoped that those at each level of operation will be clear what their responsibilities are and not interfere unduly in the detailed work of the tier(s) below once broad targets are agreed and the necessary resources provided.

EARLY YEARS:
then, now and next

Marion Dowling

Early years education has been influenced over time by four themes: insufficiency; diversity and lack of resources. The fourth theme is commitment. Without the amazing endeavour of early years practitioners there would be fewer places for under-fives, much of the provision would be less good and provision for under-fives would not be on the political agenda today. Early years is now regarded seriously. This serious regard, however, only serves to highlight just how much remains to be done.

In the early 1960s the main theme was a lack of provision. Early years education was defined as nursery education for children aged three to five years and took place in state nursery classes and schools. Provision was limited and demographically uneven, situated mainly in the north of England, Bristol and London. This lack was not really recognised as a problem. Indeed, until that time the main concern was dealing with the acute shortage of places and of teachers which had occurred in the statutory sector as a result of the post-war baby boom. There was also no great demand from parents. In 1967 the Plowden committee reported that only one third of parents approved of nursery education and wished it to be provided for their children. However, although there wasn't very much of it, the provision that existed was reasonably homogenous.

There were stringent regulations for building and staffing premises and a consistency for the aims of the provision (Webb, 1974:4). Within these parameters there were certainly beacons of excellence and British nursery schools particularly were widely visited by educationalists from overseas.

The 1960s and 1970s in a climate of optimism saw the growth of provision and the beginning of diversity. Despite this, the big expansion of nursery education recommended by the Plowden committee and promised in the white paper of 1972 never materialised. The real growth in provision was a result of the playgroup movement which snowballed from providing for one child in 1961 to approximately 170,000 in 1970 (Crowe, 1973:103). This outmatched the 100,000 children accommodated in nursery schools and classes. Nevertheless, the two provisions were regarded as quite separate and distinct. The nurseries were strongly protective of their history, regulated premises, trained staff and unique ethos. Playgroups were regarded as a community resource and a self-help group run by parents for parents. Although there was huge interest and admiration for the work undertaken by playgroups, they were essentially seen as a voluntary service; apart from token grants from the government and local authorities they made no claims on the educational budget.

In addition, a small percentage of the most needy nursery age children in the country were accommodated in social services day-care centres where the priority was family support rather than provision of early education. Yet others were accommodated in private registered nurseries and by 1990 over 6 per cent of children were with registered childminders.

Further fragmentation occurred in the 1980s with the increased admission of 4-year-olds into reception classes. Although this was happening previously – in 1971 220,000 children were in infant classes, and all but 4,000 were full-time (Webb, 1974:1) – by 1986 there was evidence to show an increasing trend to lower the admission age from five years to four. This continued, between 1983 and 1992 the number of pupils below compulsory school age in infant classes rose consistently every year. This early admission to school was (and is) completely out of line with '(EU countries, the only exceptions being Luxembourg and Holland. In the main the admission of younger children was largely unresourced, with no additional staffing and insufficient professional training. The outcome of this was that in many instances children of four years (sometimes only just four) were in a teaching group of 30 or more with one teacher, untrained to teach the age group, and no paid teaching assistant. The strong and clear recommendations for appropriate provision offered by committees of inquiry (House of Commons Education, Science and Arts Committee, 1988; DES, 1990) were not backed up by finances from government. Even where wise and sensitive recommendations were made about meeting young children's needs, as in the Rumbold report, they were not resourced and those schools that tried to respond were working on a shoestring.

By 1990 less than half of the three- and four-year-olds in England were in educational settings; of this number just under a quarter were in mainstream school where provision was invariably unsuitable (Early Childhood Statistics, 1991). Children of the same age were receiving vastly different experiences before they started statutory schooling.

The introduction of the national curriculum exacerbated difficulties for early years; it meant that resources and professional support were even more focused on the statutory sector. Apart from derogatory references to key stage 0, staff working with under-fives in reception classes and nurseries were largely ignored.

Given this gloomy background, no one could have foreseen the changes for early years which have occurred in the last five years. There was considerable scepticism when in October 1994, speaking at the Tory Party conference in Bournemouth, the Prime Minister pledged nursery places for all four-year-olds whose parents wanted them. However, action followed, namely the iniquitous voucher system. One might ask why it had taken so long to move on early years since the promise given by the same party in 1972. One major reason could be to do with the lack of clarity of the argument for more. People approached the issue from different standpoints: the need to support isolated young parents who lack help from their extended family; the need for early identification of special needs; the argument that women have the right to work, and in some cases are forced to do so as the only breadwinner; the case for the child, for promoting early cognitive and social development. Gillian Pugh, then Director of the Early Childhood Unit at the National Children's Bureau, suggested, probably rightly, that the government was finally persuaded by the law-and-order argument; the evidence from David Weikart's High Scope research (Beruetta-Clement *et al.*, 1984), which argued that pre-school education is likely to be some form of inoculation against children becoming criminals and dependent on the welfare state in later life.

The introduction of vouchers marked the start of a period of massive turmoil. The scheme was expensive and bureaucratic. It was also divisive as understandably all providers for four-year-olds competed to claim their share of the pathetically small grant of £1,100 per child for three terms worth of nursery education. Parents were confused about having to produce a voucher, particularly if it was in order for their four-year-old to attend provision in state nurseries and reception classes which had previously been available 'free'. There was also strong opposition to the fact that with so little money being made available, vouchers were being given to parents to supplement fees in private nurseries. The subsequent move to abolish vouchers in favour of grants for four-year-olds further confused matters.

The arrangements for quality assurance which led to the inspection of all voucher-funded nurseries was a major industry in itself There were many major hiccups along the way, most of them due to the huge scale of the inspection exercise, the limited funding for training and the brief time-scale allowed for implementation. The 2.5 days of training for inspectors was inadequate and most inspectors were ill-prepared for their initial inspections. One major anomaly which served to highlight difference in provision was the growth of two different types of inspection. While the new nursery inspection (Section 5) applied to all nurseries in the private, voluntary and social services domain, those in the state sector (Section 10) continued to be accountable under the schools inspection schedule (Ofsted, 1999).

There were sad casualties which arose from the Section 5 (now Section 122) inspections, notably in playgroups and private nurseries where staff were ill prepared for inspection and had no means of support to help them meet the criteria. Moreover, although the introduction of the desirable learning outcomes provided common goals for a programme for the nursery age group, there were damaging consequences to children as a result of misunderstandings. Some inspectors and providers wrongly believed that children should be expected to achieve the goals by the time they were four years of age, rather than five as was intended. As a result some children were placed under pressure to achieve standards, particularly in literacy and numeracy, often before they were developmentally ready. In addition, many providers without sufficient professional knowledge were unsure how to promote literacy and numeracy with young children and lacked support to develop expertise. Without this support, and with the best of intentions, some settings resorted to inappropriate practices, particularly in using dull and repetitive pencil-and-paper exercises to promote these outcomes. Confidence in the power of play methods waned. By using a plethora of worksheets, providers felt reassured that children were producing tangible evidence of learning.

Despite these many problems, by March 1998 10,000 nurseries which were registered for vouchers (and subsequently grants) had been inspected. Moreover, although inspection procedures were imperfect and often applied inconsistently, at least the system required all nursery settings registered for grant to be accountable for the educational provision of four-year-olds. The publication of inspection reports has also enabled parents to be better informed when selecting a pre-school place for their child. Inspections also made providers in the private sector aware of the need to plan for and assess young children's learning. Despite many of the poor practices which developed early on, overall the inspection schedule is ensuring that all settings progress in the same direction. Nursery inspectors have also had a steep learning curve. Most of those who have stayed the course are well informed and skilful in offering advice to nursery settings. Overall the quality of inspections has improved significantly and most of the resulting reports are useful to providers.

There are real grounds for optimism when one looks at the recent range of practical initiatives planned and supported by the government. The acknowledgement of the inextricable link between care and education is also important. Particularly significant is the requirement once more for local authorities to provide for children under five.. This obligation had been imposed on authorities by the 1944 Act but in fact had been breached by most local authorities. The requirement to provide had been further weakened by the 1980 Education Act, when the 'obligation' had been replaced by a 'power' which simply allowed authorities to make provision. The present requirements for early years development plans make crystal clear that responsibility for a co-ordinated service for young children lies with the local policy makers.

The early learning goals (QCA, 1999) which have replaced the desirable learning outcomes are not radical. However it is good to see that the guidance from the Qualifications and Curriculum Authority (QCA) gives more emphasis to the different needs of children. It is also heartening that the section on children's personal and social development emphasises emotional learning and includes dispositions for learning. This emphasis fits well with the inclusion of citizenship in the national curriculum. The young child's success-ful personal, social and emotional development must surely be a central and unifying aim for all early years providers; there can be nothing more important – the type of person we are colours all else that we do in life. Citizenship is also a longstanding aim of early educators. Phoebe Cusden was elected mayor of Reading in 1946; she was also head of the then Nursery Schools Association in the 1930s. In 1935 she wrote: 'The greatest contribution of the nursery school is that it is a training ground for democratic citizens – citizens who will have learned not what to think – but how to think... [The] exercise in self-reliance, unselfishness and willing co-operation, which are also features of the nursery school, will go far towards producing the kind of citizen so vitally necessary if democracy is to be capable of the tasks that devolve upon it – or even to survive' (Cusden, 1998).

Perhaps the most important QCA proposal was to restate the age range for early years which until now has been narrowly defined as three to five. The introduction of the Sure-Start programme (1999), starting with babies at three months, signals the idea of babies as a going educational concern with the ability to learn and relate to others. The proposal to extend the early years, or foundation stage of learning to the end of the reception year brings it into line with admission policies in other European countries. Certainly the extensive consultation exercise which took place indicated that the decision to extend the age range was not taken lightly. This contrasts with the decision about the admission of children taken in the House one night in 1870. A lengthy debate took place about a complicated amendment to Forster's Act, which would have established six years as the statutory age of admission. Disraeli, leader of the opposition, rose and urged the House 'to hasten on with the whole Bill... the time consuming amendment was withdrawn, the discussion of the point was concluded and the age of five went forward to reach the Statute Book'. Far from considering children's needs as the basis for the current age of admission, it appears that the decision was reached more as a consequence of Parliamentary expediency. (Szreter, 1964)

The government commitment to expansion is truly heartening. For the first time ever there is a policy to provide some nursery education for all children. Despite this, major issues remain concerning diversity and resourcing. The huge tension which remains is between diversity and quality. It is impossible to make comparisons between the state and private provision of nursery education because of the two different inspection frameworks in use. However, the first five years of nursery inspection have highlighted the differences in provision for four-year-olds, and more recently, three-year-olds, in private and voluntary nursery settings across the country. In the state sector the government-nominated centres of excellence demonstrate the high standards that can be achieved in integrating education and day care. The government is right to identify these good examples and see that they are well resourced; the ultimate aim though must be to ensure that this provision is achieved for all children.

One noticeable move towards homogeneity is the current generic use of the term 'nursery setting'. This is taken to apply to any provision registered to accept four-year-olds, As Peter Moss argued (Moss, 1992) the use of different terms in the past encouraged a fragmented

73

way of regarding young children. Nevertheless it is both dangerous and dishonest to assume that by calling everything by the same name it becomes the same. At present there are still massive differences between what the different settings provide.

Accommodation is not the major factor in achieving quality provision but minimum standards are important to support good practice. The education of young children is currently taking place in premises ranging from spacious, attractive and purpose-built accommodation to dirty church halls with inadequate storage or cramped rooms in private houses. Outside areas vary even more and in some cases do not exist.

The other aspect of diversity concerns those who educate and care for young children. Across the country there is small cohort of early years trained teachers who work largely in the state nurseries and sometimes in reception classes. Otherwise the vast majority of teachers who work with young children are not trained to do so. Most non-teachers have minimal qualifications and one in ten of those working in early years settings have no qualifications at all. There is still confusion about what an early years professional should be and what training is required. What is indisputable is that research evidence shows that the better educated the adult the better educated the children (Whitebrook, et al., 1990). The teaching role in early years settings has now become more explicit and complex. A research study of the roles of nursery teachers and nursery nurses highlighted the requirements for teaching as stated by Ofsted (Ofsted, 1995) The study concluded that where teachers are replaced by other staff (even nursery nurses who have specific expertise and knowledge) who are not qualified early years teachers, the staff require additional training in order to carry out the required teaching role. In the present circumstances, in which qualifications are so variable, it is risible to pretend that children under six will receive an equal entitlement to a quality early years education. Moreover, in adequate facilities for training devalues staff and the work that they do.

Young children's right to quality education and care is dependent on the honest recognition of the present diversity that exists. This would be made apparent through a more rigorous and single form of inspection which applies to both state, private and voluntary provision. Inspection is also no good as a tool for improvement unless it is accompanied by support. The commitment to improve remains vital, but all early educators require access to training and advice in order to help them to recognise good practice and understand how to achieve it. There is so much known now about how young children learn and how this might best be promoted. Some powerful messages have been offered for example through the Effective Early Learning project (EEL) where practitioners have been helped to observe children and identify, among other things, their levels of involvement in activities. (Pascal and Bertram, 1994) Other work has focused on young children's schemes of thinking (Nutbrown, 1994) and the role of play in promoting learning (Wood and Attfield, 1996). Dissemination remains a problem though. While some practitioners are very aware of the theoretical underpinning for their work, others simply base their practice on pragmatism. Until the implications of research studies for practice are made more widely available and understood by all practitioners, the selective use of this knowledge will only reinforce diversity.

For years, early years education has suffered from neglect, confused thinking and marginalisation. In Early Excellence, its policy document published just before the 1997 election, the Labour Party presented its vision of an early years service, integrated and coherent, accessible and affordable. Recent moves are significant in developing early years education in order to achieve these aims:

- an increasing number of authorities are providing, through their partnerships, the means for nursery settings to work together and benefit from the involvement of early years advisory teachers;

- the DfEE has added to training opportunities by providing distance learning materials to help practitioners at all levels to implement the early learning goals;

- there are proposals for a framework of qualifications and training for all adults working with young children.

There are also moves to take a hard look at the different provisions in place. The large-scale longitudinal study funded by the DfEE (the EPPE Project) aims, among other things, to establish whether some nursery settings are more effective than others in promoting children's intellectual and personal and social development during the years three to seven (Melhuish *et al.*, 1997). The project findings will be complete in 2003 but already early evidence emphasises the difference in the impact of different forms of provision. It is no surprise that state nursery schools and classes are highlighted as providing the best quality for young families. This is rightly largely attributed to better quality of trained staff and resources (Frean, 2000).

The government has taken an important step in funding this project; hopefully the study will provide evidence of what form of education is best for young children. Yet the great challenge in the next century is for politicians to use this evidence as a means of influencing other provision. This must not be forgotten in the forthcoming moves to regulate all provision for children of nought to five years by 2001. It remains to be seen how the 'new arm' of Ofsted, the nominated regulator, will deal with its vast task. There is a recognised need for a unified and coherent system. Nevertheless, this must not be at the expense of disregarding the huge differences in the providers, who will range from staff in independent schools to childminders.

The commitment of early years practitioners has continued through the dark ages and remains for the bewildering array of change which now confronts them. However, the will to provide all young children with the best form of education and care ultimately depends on society.

> But neither 'society' nor 'social attitudes' can ultimately let individuals off their own moral obligations, because there is no society that is separate from us. The whole complicated, conservative, consumerist collective is nothing but the children we were, the children we have had, the children we have now and those they will have in the future. The people who work, care and are cared for are the same people. There is nobody else to turn the social tide. (Leach, 1997:265)

References

Beruetta-Clement, J., Schweinhart, L. J., Barneff, W.S., Epstein, A.S., and Weikart, D. P., (1984) Changed lives: the effects of the Perry pre-school programme on youths through age 19, Monographs of the High/Scope Educational Research Foundation, no. 8

Crowe, B. (1973) The Playgroup Movement, London: Allen and Unwin.

Cusden, P. quoted in Dixon, A. (1998) Training for Democracy in TES, Primary Section, 20.1.98

DES (1990) Starting with Quality: The Report of the Committee of Inquiry into the Quality of the Educational Experience offered to 3- and 4-year-olds, London: Her Majesty's Stationery Office

Early Childhood Statistics (1991) Underfives in England: population and use of services, London: Her Majesty's Stationery Office

Frean, A. (2000) 'Care in private nurseries 'inferior' in The Times, 22.1.2000.

House of Commons Education, Science and Arts Committee (1988) Educational Provision for the Under-Fives – Final Report, London: Her Majesty's Stationery Office

Labour Party (1997) Early Excellence

Leach, P. (1997) Children First, Michael Joseph.

Melhuish, E., Sammons, P., Siraj-Blatchford, I., and Sylva, K. (1997) The Effective Provision of Pre-School Education Project, ongoing.

Moss, P. (1992) Perspectives from Europe in G. Pugh (ed) Contemporary Issues in the Early Years. London: National Children's Bureau.

Nutbrown, C. (1994) Threads of Thinking. London: Paul Chapman

Ofsted (1998) The Ofsted Handbook. Guidance on the Inspection of Nursery Education Provision in the Private, Voluntary and Independent Sectors. London: Her Majesty's Stationery Office

Ofsted (1999) Handbook for Inspecting Primary and Nursery Schools. London: Her Majesty's Stationery Office

Pascal, C, Bertram, A.D. and Ramsden, F. (1994) Effective Early Learning. The Quality Evaluation and Development Process. Worcester: Amber Publications.

Plowden Report. (1967) Children and their Primary Schools. London: Her Majesty's Stationery Office

Qualifications and Curriculum Authority (1999) Early Learning Goals. London: QCA Publications.

Szreter, R. (1964) 'The origins of full-time compulsory schooling at five', B.J. Educational Studies XIII:1.

Webb, L. (1974) Purpose and Practice in Nursery Education, Oxford: Blackwell.

Whitebrook, M., Howes, C. and. Phillips, D. (1990) Who Cares? Child Care Teachers and Quality of Care in America (Report of the Child Care Staffing Study), Childcare Employee Project, Oakland.

Wood, E. and Attfield, J. (1996) Play, Learning and the Early Childhood Curriculum, Paul Chapman

CHARLOTTE'S WEB:
special educational needs in mainstream schools
Ann Lewis

Introduction

I have focused this review around key books – key in the sense that each of them illustrates a particular theoretical orientation to responding to pupils with special needs, particularly those in mainstream classes. 'Special needs' is used here as a shorthand to refer to those pupils whom teachers find hard to teach. The chapter concludes with a brief, speculative, pen portrait of a projected day in the life of Charlotte, a SENCO (Special Educational Needs Co-ordinator), a decade hence.

Elaborating difference: medical and psycho-medical perspectives

In the early part of the twentieth century, provision for pupils with special needs was dominated by the idea of defects. The defect was perceived as unalterable. This went alongside the view that, in general, children with 'defects' would benefit from provision separate from that for other children. Subsequently, the 1944 Act established eleven categories of 'handicap' and some, but limited, recognition of the benefits of mainstream provision for some of these pupils.

In this context it is not surprising that the dominant theoretical orientation in the 1950s to pupils with special needs was medical or biological. A similar, psycho-medical, orientation stemmed from the work on mental testing by early psychologists, notably Burt and Cassell. Both orientations are now often referred to, more loosely, as 'the medical model'. Jeff Bailey (1998) notes that there is considerable confusion about what the term 'medical model' means. It appears to be characterised by a focus on pathology rather than normalcy, sickness rather than well-being, and an examination of the nature and aetiology of the presenting problem. Criticisms of the medical model centre on the objectifing or dehumanising of the patient/pupil; the use of positivist, scientific methods to extrapolate cause and effect relationships between symptoms and treatment; and the process of medicalisation whereby clusters of vague symptoms are organised into categories of disease. It has become fashionable to attack the medical model, but Jeff Bailey draws attention to its possible strengths. These include a careful study of the problem in order to find causes, intervention to bring about change, rigorous evaluation of intervention and long term follow-up.

Schonell's Diagnosis and Remedial Teaching in Arithmetic was published in 1958 but linked closely with his much earlier Backwardness in the Basic Subjects (1942). These drew on the psychometric work of Cyril Burt and illustrate the 'medical model' as described by Jeff Bailey. For Schonell, medical problems were a significant factor in low attainment. He cited 'malnutrition, infection of the nervous system, and the after effects of infectious diseases' as impeding normal progress in school' (1942: 43). Schonell distinguished between the 'innately dull' whose 'dullness' was caused by 'inborn mental deficiency', the 'generally backward' (who were 'remediable') and the 'specifically backward'. These are the forerunners of the distinctions in the Warnock report (DES, 1978) between severe, mild or moderate, and specific learning difficulties.

The psycho-medical orientation was also evident in the many tests and intervention programmes that sought to identify deficits in psychological processes and to remedy these as a way of attaining target tasks, usually reading. For example, there were several visual training programmes, encompassing visual sequencing (e.g. recalling the correct sequence of a series of pictures), visual motor skills (e.g. tracing shapes), figure-ground perception (e.g. distinguishing a particular shape within a mix of lines) etc. Despite extensive research endeavour, children gained proficiency in the subskills, but this did not transfer to reading. There were also attempts to 'train the brain' by correcting crossed laterality (mixed dominance of right and left sides of the body, e.g. kicking with the left foot but writing with the right hand) through physical crawling exercises. These too failed to improve cognition.

Although the medical model was in retreat in the 1980s and early 1990s, it is now resurfacing, this time in relation to dyslexia and ADHD/ADD (attention deficit hyperactivity disorder/attention deficit disorder). The features of the medical model can be readily seen to apply to these 'conditions'. In particular, clusters of symptoms are grouped to constitute specific disorders. This medicalisation of the learning or behavioural difficulties turns them into pathologies residing firmly within the child, not in the learning context. Roger Slee (1998), describing ADHD, talks of it as being transformed from pupil disruption to pupil dysfunction. It is beyond the scope of this brief review to examlne this position in detail but some of the difficulties with these applications of the medical model concern incidence and intervention. Rates of both dyslexia and ADHD vary markedly by region, social class, age and gender. For example, both dyslexia and ADHD are over-represented in boys. This is reasonable if these conditions are tied to 'maleness' genetically, but if this is not the case then social or cultural factors have to explain this bias.

There may be advantages in this medicalisation in terms of attracting finding and scarce resources for education. It may also be that some parents, teachers and children find learning difficulties easier to 'accept' if a 'medical' label is applied. There is also an obvious benefit for drug companies if a particular medication (e.g. Ritalin) becomes the routine prescription for a collection of apparently increasingly common symptoms. Matching these diagnoses with effective intervention is still problematic: 'treatments' do not always work.

Behaviourist approaches

During the 1960s and 1970s work with pupils with special needs began to be dominated by the application of behaviourist psychology. This relied on operant conditioning principles: a shorthand guide to planning teaching, very popular at the time, was ABC – Antecedent > Behaviour > Consequence. Such approaches stressed the importance of focusing on what was observable and dealing with that. They rejected medical explanations for learning difficulties or hypothesised deficits in psychological processes such as visuo-motor processing (as in tracing a line through a maze) or auditory sequential memory (as in recalling strings of digits in reverse order). Although the exclusive emphasis on the observable was a major weakness, this work was important in stressing modifiability a profoundly positive approach to teaching pupils with special needs. It also placed responsibility for progress firmly with the teacher.

Interestingly, some computer software used now with pupils with special needs has a very strong behavourist base. This is obvious in programs focusing on drill and practice routines. It is less obvious in complex software systems such as some Integrated Learning Systems. Some of these encompass very direct borrowing of behaviourism-derived sequences of small steps in tasks and frequent positive reinforcement (see BECTA, 1998; Lewis, 1997a for recent reviews of these programs).

In spite of my resistance: I've learned from children by Tom Levitt (1977) illustrated this very focused but positive approach to working with pupils with special needs. Levitt's book had its heart unapologetically on its sleeve and concluded: 'Children's potential, we all know, is immeasurable' (1977: 225). He stressed 'the essential simplicity', and hence accessibility, of behaviourist procedures. Thus the teaching techniques were demystified and the specialness of such techniques eroded. In this sense Levitt's message was very empowering, not only for teachers in specialised settings, but for mainstream teachers too. If techniques for teaching pupils with special needs were not obscure, highly technical or open only to the initiated then any teacher could carry them out. Such messages paved the way for the increased inclusion of pupils with special needs.

The behaviourist approaches were highly effective in certain contexts, in particular mechanical and self-help skills such as learning to tie shoelaces. They were much less effective in more complex tasks requiring understanding, innovation or reorganisation of knowledge. For example, there were many unsuccessful attempts to define teaching plans for creative writing based on predefined linear hierarchies of sub-skills.

Neo-behaviourists (e.g. Molloy, 1985) attempted to meet some of the criticisms of behaviourist approaches by giving some place to 'cognitive mediation'. This attempted to explain how, for example, memory of failure might inhibit children from reading words correctly despite being consistently praised when they did so. It was recognised that children were responding not to some neutral event in teaching but to their perceptions of that event. So for an adolescent with learning difficulties, receiving praise from the teacher for correct answers might be perceived by the pupil as embarrassing rather than encouraging. Thus the positive reinforcement (praise) might be counter-productive.

Cognitive orientation

Constructivist or cognitive approaches to examining learning difficulties also reflected a shift to a focus on cognition and away from reinforcement schedules of surface behaviours. Two books reflecting this orientation were Cognitive Strategies for Special Education (Adrian Ashman and Robert Conway, 1989) and Children's Learning Difficulties: A Cognitive Approach (Julie Dockrell and John McShane, 1993). These writers were interested in a cognitive task analysis. This led to a focus on the importance of examining types of error made, ways to generalise learning, and the roles of specific types of feedback. There was much related work on metacognition, that is, the ways in which children reflected on their learning. This was part of the rationale for the development of peer tutoring which involved pupils articulating what they were doing and so 'cementing' and extending their learning. Children with learning difficulties were found to benefit particularly from working as tutors to other children (see Topping, 1988). This is likely to have been due to the emotional and social benefits as well as the cognitive processes.

Bridging these individualist and the following sociological orientations is work drawing on Vygotsky's ideas which has similarly
stressed cognitive processes, albeit in the wider cultural and social
context of interaction with the teacher. This work (e.g. Rogoff, 1990;
Daniels, 1996) focused on the nature of guided participation through
which learning occurred. Applications of this perspective are illustrated in analyses of how and why individual pupils with learning
difficulties interacted with computer-based Integrated Learning
Systems. For example, in my work with children with learning difficulties I found that they believed the computer never made mistakes,
so when the computer feedback told the child the answer was wrong,
the child accepted this even though it was not always the case. For
example, a child who entered 3 in the tens column when asked to
add 15 and 15 was immediately told this was wrong; the computer
required the child to enter the units column first (discussed further
in Lewis, 1997a). This kind of feedback leads to the child developing
particular views about their capability (e.g. 'I'm bad at these sums')
and in turn to decreased motivation for further tasks.

All these three orientations focused primarily on the individual
pupil. They provided an unequivocal concern with the individual,
without getting drawn into other, possibly tangential, factors leading
to low attainment. However they may be criticised for being reduc-
tionist, labelling the learning difficulty as a discrete phenomenon,
reflecting an implicit diagnosis-remediation model, being deficit-
driven, promoting narrow school-based learning goals and assuming
a 'right' way to teach. In contrast to these individualist orientations,
in the 1980s more socially-oriented conceptions of learning difficulties were developing.

Socio-structural orientation

Sally Tomlinson's seminal work in the early 1980s (1981, 1982)
drew attention to issues concerning structural social processes
whereby some groups were marginalised and others advantaged. For
example, examination of the ethnicity and sex of pupils in special
schools for pupils with moderate learning difficulties showed that
ethnic minorities and boys were over-represented. Similarly, more
recent work has shown how the ways in which schools choose to

allocate discretionary elements of special needs budgets has 'favoured' boys (Daniels *et al*, 1998). The underlying theme of these sets of work was that 'special needs' was about structures that kept some children 'down', rather than about problems intrinsic to the child. The ways in which power and control were exercised in society led to the powerful groups developing mechanisms that reinforced their own positions. A more radical form of this position was reflected in work by Abberley (1987). He proposed a social theory of disablement in which schools, whose main task was to produce a labour force, generated curricula aimed at fulfilling this role. In this scenario, pupils unlikely to be a useful part of the labour force were removed from these curricula, i.e. these pupils were oppressed through control of the curriculum.

Disabled people writing of their experiences have informed these perspectives (e.g. Donna Williams Nobody Nowhere, 1992). She described her autistic behaviours in the early years of secondary schooling:

> I would hold my breath and tense up my stomach muscles, exerting inner pressure on myself, until I turned red, shook and fainted. The other students laughed and called me crazy. The teacher thought I was badly disturbed. I felt that I had not asked for 'their world', I had no desire to participate in it, if I had to, it would be on my terms ... I learned to dislike maths as I had always done the working out in my head but was now being told to 'show the working out'. I simply took the answers out of the back of the book and transferred them to the paper, as a compromise. (p.48)

Such accounts, and the work of disabled academics in special education (such as Tom Shakespeare, Mike Oliver and Vic Finkelstein), have raised fundamental questions about power structures and disability.

Socio-linguistic orientation

Another means whereby the powerful groups secured their positions was seen to be through language. Jenny Corbett's Bad-Mouthing (1996) is a thought-provoking illustration of work exploring the language of 'special needs'. She noted, 'This universal discourse [i.e. conventional accounts of special needs] implies that there is a single track to educational fulfilment, whereby they can join our literature' (p.97) (emphasis as in original). Awareness of the way language reveals 'confidence, caution, commitment or doubt' has led to recurrent changes in terminology such as 'retarded', 'mentally defective', 'having special needs', 'oppressed', 'differently abled' etc.

Systems-based orientation

A further politico-sociological orientation to pupils with special needs has been that which focuses on schools as systems. Here analysis is focused on the level of the institution rather than on the wider social, political or cultural systems (as in Abberley's work). From this perspective, when social institutions such as schools or LEAs generate failure, then the system produces a mechanism to deal with the failure without disrupting the institution. Thus the smooth running of the education system required that those who did not fit in were removed. This has been a very strong theme in work by Tom Skitic (1991, 1995) who described special education provision as existing in order to legitimise the mainstream. That is, special education provision exists to hide the failures of the mainstream. Similar frameworks have been used to explain how and why 'maladjusted' children, later redesignated 'children with challenging behaviours' (reflecting a move from labelling the whole child to labelling the 'aberration'), have been moved out of mainstream schools and classes. This orientation is highlighted in recent debates about pupils designated as having ADHD (Slee, 1998) and contrasts with the 'medical model' applied to these children, described earlier.

In the same way, the 1981 Education Act and 1994 Code of Practice on special educational needs have been interpreted as mechanisms to sustain the mainstream structures, rather than to radically change them, and ostensible addressing of individual 'needs' is merely a smokescreen. Related to this, writers such as Mel Ainscow (1991) describe the identification of pupils with special educational needs as indicative of the need for school reform. A similar point was made about the ways in which modification or disapplication of the national curriculum for pupils with special needs showed weaknesses in the conceptualisation of that curriculum for all children (Lewis, 1995, 1997b).

All three sociological orientations view special needs as socially produced rather than as existing independently. This is clearly in marked contrast to the individualistic orientations described earlier. The sociological orientations under- emphasise the complexity of the structures sustaining the status quo and say little about the pragmatic issue of what they mean for the teacher 'on the ground' confronted with a pupil who is not learning to read or is abusive towards other pupils. Some writers, such as Susan Hart (1996) and John Quicke (1990), have described the implications of this orientation. Much of this work focuses on changing teacher and pupil attitudes as these are seen as sustaining the old structures.

Retrospect and prospect

Each of the orientations described gave a valuable and highly focused, but partial, view. These summaries do not do justice to their complexity and heterogeneity. However they do illustrate the tremendous richness and diversity of thinking about pupils with special needs over the latter part of the twentieth century. Although I have presented these in a broadly sequential framework, writing and curriculum development at the start of the twenty-first century can be seen to reflect each of these orientations, so they are now co-existing rather than chronological.

An holistic orientation sees learners and teachers in the total context of their cognitive strengths and limitations, emotions and attitudes, and classroom, school, family and cultural contexts. This is less clear-cut than looking in detail at constituent parts. Similarly, Guy Claxton, in Hare Brain, Tortoise Mind (1997) (sub-titled 'Why intelligence increases when you think less') argues for an acceptance of ambiguity and paradox. In the special needs context this means recognising that elements from all the orientations have something to offer, although the resultant picture is much messier than a dogmatic adherence to any one of those positions.

Elements within a more holistic view of special needs might include:

1. recognition of the two-way nature of learning, i.e. that the learner (at all levels) brings things to the learning situation as well as taking something from that situation;

2. recognition that the same applies to the teacher – 'neediness' may be with the teacher rather than the learner;

3. recognition of the validity of both individuality (uniqueness) and commonality in pedagogy;

4. recognition of fluidity as inherent in attainments, interests and motivation;

5. understanding that different aspects of learner and teacher will interact, possibly in unique ways;

6. reference to a wide spectrum of learning including social, emotional, spiritual and moral aspects.

These features inevitably reflect the present: an emphasis on sub-jectivity, uncertainty, individuality, self-scrutiny and plurality with both a distrust of, and a yearning for, single-solution 'experts'. When anyone can access the Internet and its unregulated cornucopia of possible solutions, how will one 'special needs' approach be deemed to be better or worse than another? Paradoxically, un-certainty and plurality point to the need for professionals to be even better informed and clearer about what they believe and why. So systematic and balanced analyses of 'what works' in education are likely to be sought. My guess is that these will be both 'top down' and 'bottom up'. The former are reflected in the DfEE's com-missioned research reviews (e.g into autism (Jordan *et al.*, 1998), the education of deaf pupils (Powers *et al.*, 1998) and provision for pupils with moderate learning difficulties (Dyson *et al.*, 1999)) and the British Educational Research Association's examination of 'sen pedagogy' (Lewis and Norwich, 2000; Norwich and Lewis (in press)). I suspect that we shall have more such reviews and attempts to draw out implications for classroom practice. Complementing these, we need 'bottom up examination of what works for pupils with special educational needs, examining the processes (individual, interpersonal and contextual) involved in a bout of learning. Whatever emerges will not be the definitive orientation towards special needs but will become part of the continuing evolution of theory and practice. I end this chapter with speculation about what this might look like 'on the ground'.

Fast forward to 2010

Charlotte trained to teach in the late 1990s. At that time support work (or 'special needs' as it was called then) got only a brief coverage in the course and most of that was on IEPs (individual education programmes), something we don't hear about at all now. After university Charlotte went abroad and worked in Chile for a couple of years. She wasn't sure about going in for primary teaching but still, the pay was good and respect for the profession had grown since the 1980s. Lots of people did some teaching now, at least for a few years between other things. She'd been teaching for five years before she got this latest job – support manager (what used to be called a SENCO) in a large primary school. Her friend Chris had a similar job but he was support manager for a cluster of small primaries. They had both been selected, while at university, for 'accelerated careers'.

Charlotte's day always began with checking the Support Bank. This was funded by Brussels – a huge online library of resources, hints, lesson ideas, teachers' magazines, national and European press releases, work plans, room layouts, directories of advisers and much more. There was a small fee each year but it was worth it, especially when you were new to the job as she was. The online experts provided a good service and there was a guarantee of an answer to your query within five minutes. It might come from anywhere in the world. That's how things were now; supported children had the same sorts of needs, in many ways, whatever their country.

After that, Charlotte had time with her two support officers. They did all the checking and keeping of records on supported children plus handling the appointments between Charlotte and all the people she worked with in planning the children's programmes. It was a large job but made easier by the Internet communication between everyone. A few of the parents had to go to the local 'info centre' in the supermarket to send and pick up messages but it worked quite well. One of the support officers, Loonor, was a maths graduate, which was very useful as she could process all the statistical data. She was building up evidence about how particular programmes were working with individual children. The manufacturers were interested and the school sold the data to them as part of the firm's Rand D programme. The European authorities were interested too, there was similar work going on all over the world and there was evidence about how, across different cultures, boys needed different approaches from girls at certain ages. Leonor used the information as part of her professional development programme and was hoping to get her Ed.D. soon for the portfolio of development projects she'd built up. This work had been monitored by the e-university based in the English Midlands. The other support officer, Nihat, had very good skills in European languages, so he did a lot of the liaison with Brussels and colleagues from mainland Europe.

During the morning various children came to the Support Centre in which Charlotte, Leonor and Nihat were based, to get their medication. One wall was taken up with the medicab. This was a 'smart' medicine cabinet which automatically dispensed the right dosage of the right medication to the right child at the right time. A lot of the children were on Ritalix (a smaller version of the old Ritalin), which was dispensed in very small capsules. This meant that dosages could be varied daily by the health centre and the information relayed to the medicab. Increasingly children needed to take medication for epilepsy, asthma and diabetes so the range of drugs given out at school was growing rapidly in number and range. The medicab automatically double-checked that no dangerous combinations of drugs were being issued.

After the lunchtime break it was time for Charlotte to check on the children's 'motor hour'. So many children were coming into school with physical problems (dyspraxia, coordination difficulties and general lack of stamina) that most schools now had this 'tone-n-grow' session. It was fun and popular with the children as light, sounds and movement were all synchronised and light/sound effects were activated by the child's body movements.

The old literacy and numeracy hours had been gradually abandoned. They were still there but so much a part of the fabric of the school day that they didn't need to be identified specifically. There were demands for an arts and culture hour in every primary school. The new interest in folk and ethnic arts from around Europe and beyond fuelled this. But nobody had yet sorted out how best to address the spiritual needs of supported children. A lot of the new work in the support field was focusing on spirituality and the arts as the late 1990s curriculum looked too narrow and there was more emphasis on children's 'all round' development.

During the afternoon Charlotte had to update the contacts lists from the Directory of Providers in Education (DOPIE). A lot of the old LEA inspectors, advisers and educational psychologists were still in the directory but there were many new consultants too. Each had his or her own specialism: massage, yoga, Alexander technique, aroma-therapy, group work, psychotherapy etc. Many of these people had non-education backgrounds but that increased the range of ideas. There was a large market for the services and pricing was com-petitive. One of Nihat's jobs was to obtain competitive costings for the services to the school. The LEA had been replaced by a regional body which had far fewer powers, so only the more infrequent dis-abilities had any regional coordination; otherwise each school sorted out its own provision. Special needs monies were identified in the budget and it was up to the school to choose how to use them.

Anyone wanting to work in the school had to take the CUDDly test (Cognitive Understanding of Disabilities and Difficulties) – that was a sign of how far social attitudes were seen as important to schools' targets. A task for the afternoon for Charlotte was the ecosystemic audit; a kind of health check on the school's climate and ethos. This was a series of checks which she did each week (for example, reviewing the location of resources so that this was not disadvantag-ing particular children). Possible changes were discussed with the staff; flooring was an issue because of the repercussions for partially hearing children as well as those with physical disabilities. There were recurrent team discussions about more zoning to help with this but some staff felt that this would bring a return to the old segre-gation of the last millennium.

By then it was time for Charlotte to finish for the day. She hadn't taught any children; she was not involved in that side of things any longer. Most of the supported children were taught for at least part of the time by a series of support trainers (nicknamed 'the saints').

91

Charlotte was not planning on staying in support work but it was a good stepping stone to setting up her own company. Alternatively, the people and organisational skills she'd developed through support were much sought after and she could command a high salary, anywhere in the English-speaking world, with one of the many freelance consultancy or inspection firms.

References

Abberley, P. (1987) 'The concept of oppression and the development of a social theory of disability' Disability, Handicap and Society 2 115-19

Ainscow, M. (Ed) (1991) Effective Schools for All London: David Fulton

Ashman, A.F. and Conway, R.N.F. (1989) Cognitive Strategies for Special Education London: Routledge

Bailey, J. (1998) Medical and psychological models in special needs education 44-60 in C. Clark, Dyson, D. And Millward, A. (Eds) Theorising Special Education London: Routledge

BECTA (1998) The UK Integrated Learning Systems evaluations: Final report Coventry: BECTA

Claxton, G. (1998) Hare Brain Tortoise Mind London: Fourth Estate

Corbett, J. (1996) Bad-Mouthing London: Falmer

Daniels, H. (Ed) (1996) An Introduction to Vygotsky London: Routledge

Daniels, H., Vey, V., Leonard, D. And Smith, M (1998) Issues of equity in special needs education as seen from the perspective of gender, mimeo. Birmingham: University of Birmingham

DES (1978) Special Educational Needs (The Warnock Report) London: HMSO

Dockrell, J. and McShane, J. (1994) Children's Learning Difficulties: a cognitive approach Oxford: Blackwell

Dyson, A. et al (1999) Costs and outcomes for pupils with MLD in special and mainstream schools London: DfEE

Hart, S. (1996) Beyond Special Needs London: Paul Chapman

Jordan, R., Jones, G. And Murray, D. (1998) Educational interventions for children with autism: a literature review of recent and current research London: DfEE

Lewis, A. (1995) Primary Special Needs and the National Curriculum 2nd edn. London: Routledge

Lewis, A. (1997a) Integrated Learning Systems and pupils with special educational needs pp.103-117 in J. Underwood and J. Brown (eds.) Integrated Learning Systems Potential into Practice London: NCET Heinemann

Lewis, A. (1997b) The National Curriculum and children with SEN in mainstream primary schools in Developing the primary school curriculum: the next steps London: SCAA

Lewis, A. and Norwich, B. (2000) Mapping a Pedagogy for Special Educational Needs Exeter: University of Exeter, School of Education.

Levitt, T. (1977) In spite of my resistance: I've learned from children New York: Merrill

Molloy (1985) cited in Ashman and Conway

Norwich, B. and Lewis, A. (in press) Mapping a Pedagogy for Special Educational Needs British Educational Research Journal

Powers, S., Gregory, S. and Thoutenhoofd, E.D. (1998) The educational achievements of deaf children London: DFEE

Quicke, J., Beasley, K. and Morrison, C. (1990) Challenging prejudice through education Lewes: Falmer

Rogoff, B. (1990) Apprenticeship in Thinking Oxford: Oxford University Press

Schonell, F.J. (1942) Backwardness in the Basic Subjects London: Oliver and Boyd

Schonell, F.J. (1958) Diagnosis and Remedial Teaching in Arithmetic London: Oliver and Boyd

Skitic, T. (1991) Behind Special Education Denver: Love Publications

Skitic, T. (1995) Disability and Democracy: reconstructing [special] education for post-modernity New York: Teachers College Press

Slee, R. (1998) Inclusive education? This must signify 'new times' in educational research British Journal of Educational Studies 46 4 440-454

Tomlinson, S. (1981) Educational subnormality; a study in decision making London: Routledge and Kegan Paul

Tomlinson, S. (1982) A Sociology of Special Education London: Routledge and Kegan Paul

Topping, K. (1988) The Peer Tutoring Handbook London: Croom Helm

Williams, D. (1992) Nobody Nowhere London: Transworld

Management

MODERNISING PRIMARY TEACHING:
some issues relating to performance management

R.J. Campbell

Professional culture and curriculum reform

Research in the 1990s (Campbell and Neill, 1994a, 1994b, 1994c; Evans *et al.*, 1994) raised three dilemmas for teachers arising from the conventional professional culture of primary teaching which were working against the objectives of the post-1988 reform agenda. The first was that teachers' conscientiousness created problems for the achievement of the strictly cognitive objectives of the reforms, since primary teachers' energies, efforts and time were diffused too broadly, commonly being diverted into social, welfare and affective purposes. Some (e.g. Alexander *et al.*, 1992) have seen this as a problem of professional ideology arising from primary teachers' enthusiasm for the progressive values in the Plowden report (CACE, 1967). However, as has been argued elsewhere (Campbell, 1995) as modern society fractures morally, the state needs to reinforce the social and moral functions of schooling, primarily because it remains the only common site for moral socialisation, as respect for family, church, the law and other socialisation agencies weakens.

Second, although teachers spent relatively long hours on work, a small but significant proportion of the time was spent on activities that did not require graduate qualifications, and could reasonably be carried out by para-professionals: for example, taking registers, photocopying, mounting displays, supervising children at breaks and at the beginning and end of the school sessions. That this is not merely a resource issue – though it is that – was suggested by one finding that those teachers with more classroom assistant support spent significantly more, not less, time in mounting classroom displays than those with less or no classroom support. This suggested the existence of an occupational culture which stressed collaboration on all tasks, rather than a clearer, more hierarchical, division of labour in schools; a culture of inefficiency, rendering teachers' complaints about overload and overwork less than convincing.

Third, the central government had encountered little cultural resistance from primary teachers about much of its agenda, and almost none in respect of curriculum reform. The professional response had been a commitment to making the reforms work. But as it became increasingly clear that the curriculum reforms were ill thought out, poorly managed centrally, designed to lead to reduced time on the teaching of reading at Key Stage 1, and undeliverable in the time available, teacher commitment was being undermined, giving way to cynicism.

The period since 1994 has seen these dilemmas, if anything, aggravated. The emphasis on the moral and social purposes of the school has increased, with renewed emphasis on social inclusiveness, the role of literacy and numeracy in raising pupil self-esteem, and the re-invention of the social and moral curriculum by Professor Crick's review of citizenship education. The role of primary teachers has if anything become even more diffused: in addition to teaching the curriculum, they are expected to be secretaries, social workers, community liaison officers, paramedics, priests (though the recent activities of some priests may cause us to revise that one), teacher trainers, expert spotters of drug abuse, advisers on safe sex and unsafe drugs. In addition, the Teacher Training Agency wants them to be action researchers. Cynicism in the profession about reform has been massively reinforced, primarily through the botched 're-vision' of the curriculum by Sir Ron Dearing – itself an officially sanctioned piece of cynical manipulation of curricular arithmetic – but also by the 1998 Blunkett revision of the status of the non-core foundation subjects. The latter appeared to raise questions about the benefits of the 'broad and balanced' curriculum envisaged in the 1988 Act, and to which teachers had committed enormous effort and time. Most demoralising of all, by 1998, according to the NFER (Foxman, 1998; Brooks, 1998), standards in literacy had not been raised and the long-standing decline in numeracy relative to our international competitors had not been halted. Ten years on, to a malicious chorus of 'we told you so' from the hard bitten staffroom dinosaurs, many of those who worked hardest to make the 1998 reforms work were retreating into the sullen disillusionment of reform fatigue. In 1989, a study by Professor Oswald in the Warwick Business School found teachers to be least happy and least satisfied of all workers.

The usual way of interpreting this state of affairs in the professional climate has been to see it, quite understandably, as an illustration of the Conservative government's failure to effect educational reform – chickens coming home to roost malevolently on the system. This, however, assumes that education reform, for that government, was synonymous with raised standards in the curriculum. Another view, given in an address to his department by Michael Bichard, Permanent Secretary in the DFEE, is that the UK Education Reform Acts of the late 1980s and early 1990s were good examples of the need 'to confront vested interests' (Bichard, 1999). Given the easy and now uncontested establishment of a national curriculum and testing, the weakening of LEA control, the imposition of external inspection through Ofsted and the take over of training by the Teacher Training Agency and the DFEE, on Bichard' 5 criteria the record of the previous administration has been outstandingly successful. Moreover, it enables the government's performance management proposals to be seen as an extension of this success: exploiting the fracture of the professional interest groups in order to introduce higher performance management into the system. But for the incoming Labour government, concerned above all with raising educational performance, the inheritance of widespread professional cynicism presented a daunting challenge, particularly if, as I argued above, it is now deeply embedded in the professional culture. It suggests at the very least that government, like the teachers, is facing a significant challenge. From this point of view, how far do the government's proposals face up to the problems hindering the previous reform implementation, as heralded in its ambitious reform agenda?

There are four principal elements in the modernisation process:

- a new and different career structure

- strengthened school leadership

- improved training and status

- better in-class support for teachers

Modernised career structure: freeing teachers to teach?

The new career structure is primarily designed to achieve a modern version of the three Rs: to recruit, retain and reward good teachers, enabling those who want it to concentrate on what they are excellent at: teaching pupils. High performers will be given substantial financial incentives to stay in the classroom, and to spread their model of good practice. Those who choose not to seek such status will be held at a performance threshold. Regular assessment of classroom performance of the high achievers would be made to monitor the maintenance of good-quality in teaching. The key question here is not whether performance-related pay will 'work', but whether the new culture will enable those teachers who so wish, to prioritise among the competing and diffuse demands they have previously faced, and focus more narrowly upon instructing pupils; whether paying good teachers highly will provide a much needed legitimisation for teachers to concentrate upon the cognitive. If this leads to a more 'continental' role for teachers, in which para-professionals concentrate upon the affective, it is likely to lead to a greater sense of job satisfaction for teachers. In this performance culture, electronic registers, computerised assessment and recording systems, administrative support staff; and increased numbers of classroom assistants (interestingly called 'teaching assistants' in the 1998 Green Paper) are all on offer with one prime purpose to free teachers to teach:

'teachers spend on average less than half their working time teaching face to face. Too much time is spent on administrative chores, some of which could be done better and more cost effectively by others. In general, working conditions are below the standard which well-qualified graduates in other fields take for granted.' (DfEE, 1999, para 22)

Modernised leadership: ensuring that leaders lead?

The government's performance management policy proposes to improve the financial rewards for effective school leadership, whether practised by heads or others, and to 'fast track' the most able young teachers to accelerate their rise to leadership of the profession. In return, they will need to be a more flexible part of the profession, with a longer year than those on the standard track. The contractual arrangements for heads will include the possibility of a fixed-term contract and performance-related pay set against annual targets for school improvement. Significantly enhanced high-status training arrangements, including a National College for School Leadership, are being provided. At the same time, heads who do not wish to rise to the challenge of leadership, and those judged to be under-performing, will be sidelined or sacked.

Underlying these proposals are three assumptions. First, leadership will depend on further steps toward devolved responsibility – giving heads increased freedom to manage their school autonomously, within the constraints of accountability. Successful schools will have light-touch inspections, and, echoing Excellence in Schools, 'intervention [by central government] in inverse proportion to the success of the school' will be the guiding principle.

Here the government has learnt a lesson from its predecessor's failures. The constant penetration of school management by detailed central prescription through stature had failed to raise standards: now, ambitious and high-performing leaders in schools will be, so to speak, given their head. Secondly, and presumably despite the recruitment crisis, there will be zero tolerance of poor leadership performance, alleged to characterise one in seven schools. Third, the intention to control the quality of leadership training likewise reflects the recognition that previous training, largely managed by the LEAs and the Teacher Training Agency (TTA), was variable and often short-termist. The new training will be high quality, from leading-edge professionals in education and business; it will be life-long, and continuously refreshed in a nationally established frame-work.

Discussion: the implications of the performance culture

The government's performance management proposals seem therefore to be taking cognisance of previous difficulties, especially in its conception of a performance culture in which a greater division of labour in schools reduces the wide and unachievable role expectations currently laid upon class teachers; in which high-quality instruction, undiverted into bureaucracy, is subject to constant appraisal and financially rewarded; and in which effective school leadership is recognised and supported by good training. Running through the text, mantra-like, is the rhetoric of modernisation, nowhere defined. Three principal themes are embodied in the rhetoric: the secularisation of teacher motivation, technology-driven specialisation of function, and contractual flexibility.

The secularisation of teacher motivation

I have already characterised the existing primary school culture as not performance-oriented, drawing attention to the vocationally driven motivation that typifies primary teachers' reasons for entering the profession, with primary teaching modelled on a substitute mother-figure role, in which the satisfactions of nurturing combine with an inclination to sacrifice personal interests to those of the child (see Steedman, undated). Very recently, Stagg (1999), examining the motivation of career changers contemplating a switch into teaching, found a similar altruism, reflected in career changers' desire to 'put something back into society'. This quasi-religious motivation can be traced to the religious origins of schooling, and surfaces in the 'conscientiousness syndrome (Campbell and Neill, 1994c) associated with a predominantly female workforce, with apparently lower career aspirations and demonstrably lower occupational achievement than those of its few male counterparts. The performance management arrangements, which are concerned with recruitment, retention and reward, seek to secularise teachers' motivation: to give emphasis to the external rewards – financial incentives and high status – as a prime source of motivation for the leading-edge professionals, parallel to the motivation operating on other graduates currently choosing a career in the financial services, business and law.

A restructuring of this highly feminised character of teacher motivation will be immensely difficult to achieve, since it will require a change in one of the enduring and fundamental characteristics of the profession. It may be much harder in primary than in secondary teaching. High levels of conscientiousness, genuine and reciprocated affection for young children, and long hours of work may be necessary, but will no longer be sufficient. In the performance culture, demonstrable increases in pupils' learning are what will be rewarded, measured through a carefully constructed appraisal mechanism. The rather desperate attempt by the TTA to recruit more men into primary teaching may be an implicit acknowledgement of the size of the cultural problem.

There has already been a predictable opposition from unions and some academics to performance-related pay: it will be divisive; it has been shown not to work in the private sector settings; appraisal and measurement of performance is an unreliable art; and performance indicators (Ofsted reports and test results) are crude. The fast trackers might also come to be seen as a privileged elite, given that a 5 per cent maximum are envisaged to be fast tracked. It is pretty certain that the profession is due for some turbulence, and that primary schools as small organisations can tolerate relatively little professional conflict and envy. Parents might react badly when their children don't get the high performing teachers. But the proof of this particular pudding really will be in its eating. Whether professional motivation will be changed by attraction to Mammon is an empirical question. But the performance culture is an attempt to lever the profession out of its traditional, cosy, intrinsic, quasi-religious, feminised, vocation-oriented motivation – a motivation which renders the profession open to exploitation – into a motivation more responsive to external rewards and sanctions. The performance culture assumes what we might call the secularisation of the profession. The new teachers will be attracted to an occupation where they will be judged on the effectiveness of their skills rather than on the warmth of their relationships with children.

Technology-driven specialisation of function

There has been a constant picture from research into primary teaching in this country of overworked class teachers, with not enough time, and inadequate support, to achieve the objectives set for them. The conscientious primary teacher writes her own worksheets, manages the whole class while dealing with individuals, sorts out the class computer when it crashes and still manages to make frequent changes to her wall displays. A technology of support for her is proposed in the 1998 green paper: Information and Communication Technologies (ICT) systems and training, teaching assistants, technical and clerical assistance, electronic registers and computer-based records. This technology has one overriding purpose; to make her more efficient as a teacher.

As Alexander (1984) has pointed out, the conception of the generalist class teacher has hardly changed since its invention in the late nineteenth century as a cheap mechanism for the delivery of mass education. The generalist class teacher has been expected to care for the whole child, looking after the health, safety and welfare of children as well as teaching them the whole curriculum. This conception was both non-specialised and inefficient and may have contributed both to the poor performance of English primary pupils in international comparisons of educational attainment, and to the low status of primary teaching. With the kind of technology-driven efficiency proposed, the teacher has to become not merely more efficient, but also more specialised in function; someone else deals with grazed knees, mounts wall displays, supports the learning of individuals, fixes the computer and maintains the records, while she concentrates on the narrow performance curriculum.

This restructuring of the role will prove difficult, since it too requires a change in occupational culture. Primary teachers will have to learn to let go of many activities which keep them busy but do not contribute to pupil learning. (There is also a somewhat romantic treatment of ICT in the 1998 green paper, as though the effectiveness of ICT-associated pedagogy were already well established.) Overworked and stressed teachers should ultimately be the principal beneficiaries of these proposals; but the proposals will also remove from teachers one of their current excuses for poor pupil performance.

Contractual flexibility

The conventional approach to employment in the teaching profession has been the permanent contract, which the teacher loses only by choice or from demonstrated moral turpitude – from what we must learn to call 'educative experiences'. The contract was national and uniformly applicable in the maintained sector. More recently there have been significant increases in the appointment of part-time and fixed-term contracts, although it is unclear whether this has arisen from a conscious strategy or from financial exigency. In evidence to the Select Committee on the Professional Status, Recruitment and Training of Teachers (House of Commons, 1996/7), the CBI argued that 'the pay and conditions of teachers are extremely rigid by private sector standards' and the Committee recommended differentiated payment for shortage subject teachers – in effect a step toward a more market-responsive contract.

The government's approach to performance management takes marketisation of teachers' contracts significantly beyond mere market responsiveness. For all teachers, contractual flexibility will be imposed, though in different degrees, depending upon status and responsibility. First, all teachers will be eligible to bid to cross the performance threshold, and if they do so there will be 'higher professional expectations'. Before the threshold, automatic entitlement to salary increments will be removed, and unsatisfactory teachers will be required to leave the profession – both consequences of a very hard-edged contractual flexibility.

Second, the fast-trackers would be put on supplementary contracts entailing a longer working year and greater geographical (and presumably social) mobility. This version of flexibility is designed to service the system, rather than simply reward the individual, and it must raise a question, in what will continue to be a largely female workforce, about equal opportunities to benefit from a scheme requiring regular relocation.

Third, headteachers (and other school leaders) will be paid on a leadership pay spine, with progress depending on annual performance targets, arrived at through appraisal. Location on these pay spines would remove the current contractual restrictions on working time. It is also envisaged that heads might be on fixed-term contracts, and arrangements for heads to step down from leadership to a 'less pressurised role before retirement' are being put in place. There are big carrots: primary heads' salaries will be raised to reflect their responsibilities and performance, and although there may be some resistance within the profession as a whole, the attractiveness of significantly increased salaries and faster career development will probably mean that contractual flexibility will be more easily accommodated into the professional culture than changes in motivation and specialisation.

Two problems in the transition period

Two considerations about the future development of the profession emerge from the above analysis. The first is fairly obvious, though none the less important for that. It is that the government's performance management system is based upon a gift exchange: the profession gains improved pay, training and status only insofar as it delivers on performance. This does not look, as some commentators have suggested, like the payment by results of the Elementary Code. Performance will not be measured solely by results in tests, as the Performance Management Framework (DfEE, 2000) makes clear. However, the profession is not going to get something for nothing: it is a something-for-something proposal, and positive pupil outcomes, including gains in test scores, will be among the prime indicators of teacher performance. The problem for the culture is direct: under performance management motivation and reward are individualised, not collective, except for the school performance award. In general it is not the profession, or the school but the individual performance that gets recognised and rewarded. How easily that can be accommodated into the collaborative and collegial cultures currently existing is not clear.

The second consideration is less clear and concerns those who do not join the culture of ambition. It is envisaged that a 'sizeable minority' of the profession, according to the green paper Technical Consultation Document (para. 22) will not cross the performance threshold, and will therefore be held at a fixed point on the salary spine. To those may have to be added the substantial minority of poor leaders, normally heads – one in seven according to Ofsted figures quoted (though these are, surprisingly, given the detail of the Ofsted database, referred to as Ofsted estimates). Some of these failures in the performance culture may leave the profession, or be sacked, while others will be sidelined into something less challenging. If we put to one side those who leave the profession, there will remain a large rump judged publicly to be underperforming and under-motivated (or at best anachronistically motivated) who cannot or will not operate well in the performance culture. Among them will be disproportionately the older, professionally stagnating teachers and heads. It is difficult to see what the performance management has to offer them. Being sidelined into something less challenging does not on the face of it seem either clear or attractive, unless they can all become school bursars. To note this is not to argue that such teachers should continue to be rewarded as highly as others, but it is to recognise that a significant minority of the profession will be locked into a cultural time warp in which they are seen to be losers. To put it melodramatically, it could lead to part of a generation's experience and skills in the profession being written off; and to their becoming disaffected with teaching. Such a group might be a transitional characteristic of the changes proposed, but it would become a dead-weight on the transformation of the whole profession for a considerable time – 20 years or so – to come. This is especially the case given the medium to long-term recruitment problems, which would mean that, though sidelined, they would have to be retained. There are always casualties of modernising processes, but the casualties of this particular consequence of the process may well include pupils as well as the teachers.

There will of course be initial resistance. But it is difficult to believe that the widespread cynicism, demoralisation, low status and poor recruitment in the profession at the current time can be tolerated much longer. The resisters will need to show how their plans for improving the profession will be more effective, more quickly, than those proposed by the government. The status quo really is not an option.

References

Alexander, R J (1984) Primary Teaching. London Cassell

Alexander, R J; Rose, J and Woodhead, C (1992) Curriculum Practice and Class-room Organisation in Primary Schools: A Discussion Paper. London Department of Education and Science

Bichard, M (1999) 'Modernising the Policy Process', http://ntwebl/Gen Bef Speeches/Speeches/MichaelBichard/pmpa/htm, 25.01.1999

Brooks, G (1998) 'Trends in Standards of Literacy in the UK, 1948-1996', Topic, Slough NFER

CACE (1967) Children and their Primary Schools London Her Majesty's Stationery Office

Campbell, R J (1985) 'Primary Teachers' Work: some sources of conflict between education policy and occupational culture'. Paper presented to the 8th Annual Conference of the Association for the Study of Primary Education, Southampton, September.

Campbell, R J and Neill, S (1994a) Primary Teachers at Work. London Routledge

Campbell, R J and Neill, S (1994b) Secondary Teachers at Work. London Routledge

Campbell, R J and Neill, S (1994c) Curriculum Reform at Key Stage 1: Teacher Commitment and Policy Failure. London Longman

DfEE (1998) Teachers Meeting the Challenge of Change: Green Paper and Technical Document

DfEE (2000) Performance Management in Schools

Evans, L; Packwood, A; Neill, S and Campbell, R J (1994) The Meaning of Infant Teachers' Work. London Routledge

Foxman, D (1998) 'Monitoring Trends in Numeracy in the UK, 1953-1995', Topic, Slough NFER

House of Commons (1996/7) Education and Employment Committee: The Professional Status, Recruitment and Training of Teachers. London Her Majesty's Stationery Office

Stagg, P (1999) 'Working Paper on career changers' perceptions of teaching as a career'. Centre for Education and Industry, University of Warwick.

Steedman, C (undated) 'Impeccable Governesses, National Dames and Moral Mothers mimeo, University of Warwick, Department of History

PRIMARY SCHOOL MANAGEMENT:
past, present and future
Geoff Southworth

Introduction

In this chapter I will review the changing nature of primary school management. Given the restrictions on length, I can only offer a brief overview of the major trends during the last 50 years. While there will be many issues I shall omit, I nevertheless intend to show that primary school management has developed over this period. It is also, given the Government's green paper (DfEE, 1998), poised to enter yet another new era which looks to be one of performance management.

In the first section I will outline the major trends during the last half century. I shall also set out some of the important themes around which school management has centred. Building on these themes I will then highlight three specific aspects of primary school management which I believe warrant closer examination for present and future developments. These aspects will be discussed in the second, third and fourth sections. In the fifth section I will draw together my ideas and offer a glimpse of what the future of primary school management might be.

Past and present trends

During the 1950s and 1960s very little research was conducted into primary school management. It was not regarded as a distinctive feature of schooling. Rather, management was seen as the sole responsibility of the headteacher whose personality created 'the climate

of feeling – whether of service and co-operation or of tension and uncertainty – and that establishes standards of work and conduct'
(Ministry of Education, 1959: 52). Heads were seen as the key individuals whose management style was a function of their personality.

Such an outlook was largely undisturbed by the Plowden report. It
was not until the HMI Primary Survey that a variation on this perspective began to emerge. Although the survey did not have much to
say directly about management, the emphasis placed on teachers
with special responsibilities (coordinators or subject leaders today)
encouraged LEAs to consider strengthening the role of these post
holders and to see how other staff could support the headteacher.
During the 1970s, formal interest in school management began to
appear in university courses, as well as curriculum management
courses. Much of this activity favoured secondary schools, but the
beginnings of the study of primary school management also
emerged.

In 1983 the Secretary of State for Education introduced national provision for school management training with the advent of one-term
and 20-day secondments for heads. Also around this period (late
1970s and early 1980s) a whole raft of courses was designed and
developed and school management moved to a central rather than a
peripheral position in professional development. Much of this provision was focused on headteachers, although some courses for
deputies and coordinators became common and these have continued to the present. These activities generally dealt with such
issues as decision making, school organisation, self-evaluation,
curriculum management, pastoral care and staff selection.

With the 1988 Education Act, and all that this legislation set in train
in terms of the national curriculum, Local Management of Schools
(LMS) and new powers for school governors, primary school
management began to change again. Many heads perceived the
national curriculum as meaning they had lost their perceived control
over the curriculum. Many also saw LMS as increasing the amount
of bureaucracy in schools and it was interpreted as dealing a mortal
blow to their professional leadership. In fact, LMS assuaged many
heads' feelings of a loss of control because they now had direct

influence over their schools' budgets. By 1993 the introduction of LMS was well under way, and it is safe to claim that between 1983 and 1993 we moved from school management to self-managing schools.

Over a similar timescale effective schools research began to influence policy makers' views. This research was interpreted as showing that schools need to be effective at two levels simultaneously, at the level of the school as an organisation and at the classroom level, where effective teaching and learning are vital. This interpretation led to school organisation and management matters taking even greater significance. Moreover, the research emphasised the importance of leadership and prompted increased emphasis on it.

By the early 1990s schools were also faced with many initiatives to manage. Schools had moved from a time of relative stability when change was one thing at a time, to a period of turbulence, when staff were having to deal with multiple, simultaneous changes. This state of affairs stimulated interest in school development planning and in the late 1980s and early 1990s development plans became common in virtually all schools.

The introduction of development plans on a national scale was an important trend for two reasons. First, because the widespread adoption of development plans showed how school management had become strongly concerned with the management of change. The national reforms created confusion and uncertainty in schools and many senior staff began to use development plans to help them to create some sense of order and priority. Second, the introduction of school development plans signalled increased emphasis on primary schools becoming more cohesive as organisations.

Many of these changes also triggered other developments. Teachers were now working much more collaboratively than a decade before. Joint planning became the norm, as did many more meetings and school-level policy-making. As a consequence of the increase in teacher interaction, it was soon acknowledged that school management and the process of change were either enabled or disabled by particular types of organisational and professional cultures.

Since 1988 accountabilities have also sharpened. The introduction of league tables, competition between schools, parental choice and open enrolment led many heads to take an interest in marketing and caused some to become very much more entrepreneurial in winning resources for their schools. The creation of the Office for Standards in Education (Ofsted) also dramatically altered accountabilities. Regular inspections, with reports made public (as HMI inspection reports had been since the 1980s), with schools judged to be succeeding or not, and with explicit comments about the effectiveness and efficiency of the school's leadership and management included in the report, transformed the nature and character of accountability. If it was true in the 1970s that the school curriculum had been a 'secret garden', by the mid 1990s schools were in danger of becoming public and political playgrounds.

Parental involvement in schools has also increased over the last two decades and governors are now expected to play a far more active role than formerly. Governors are required to play a part in development planning, in establishing and monitoring the school's post-inspection action plans, in appointing staff and in managing the school's budget. Community involvement, in one form or another has undoubtedly altered.

As the 1990s progressed, school improvement became a stronger emphasis. Indeed, an important shift in the language of management occurred during the mid-1990s with talk of school development giving way to concerns about improving schools. Initially this meant Ofsted-style school inspections and schools trying to monitor the value they added to pupils' learning. Evidence-based management has now become the norm. National assessments at the end of key stages, plus a variety of other measures and tests, including baseline assessments, have become established practice. These, coupled with information technology, have led to senior staff monitoring and evaluating pupils' progress and school performance. When New Labour won the 1977 election they declared that they were on a 'crusade' to improve schools and raise standards of achievement.

School improvement thinking and policy-making during the 1990s often focused on failing and weak schools. This emphasis perhaps harmed the concept of improvement in the minds of many teachers because they only understood it as a remedial exercise; you had to be poor to need to get better. Although the idea that schools need to improve on their previous best has taken longer to become established, the emphasis on failing schools demonstrated that many in education were becoming concerned at perceived levels of poor performance. Very recently, central government has begun to emphasise that alongside the need to remedy poor performance, underachieving schools will also be put under the microscope and expected to raise their standards.

Consequently, the self-managing school of the early 1990s has become the self-improving school. The next step in this journey appears to be increased emphasis on pupil, school and teacher performance. The green paper (DfEE, 1998) strongly signalled that the quality of teaching should now be a major feature of appraisal and thus of school management. Moreover, the new century has begun with the government introducing performance management into all schools. Quite how this will turn out is anyone's guess. Earlier efforts between 1988 and 1995 to introduce a developmental model of teacher appraisal failed, as much because this initiative was overtaken by many other reforms as because of any inherent flaws in the approach. Nevertheless, appraisal is back on the agenda and in a new guise which embodies contemporary interest in and concern about performance, quality and standards.

Running through these developments are a number of other themes. For example, the first 25 years of this review look to be a period of relative stability, evolution and incrementalism. The latter 25 years appear to be a time of accelerating activity and change. Also, school management has moved from a time when it was concerned with developing the school to a time when managers are now pre-eminently focusing on improvement. The former marks a time when education was largely preoccupied with process issues, while the latter is concerned with the outcomes, as well as the processes, of schooling and teaching and learning.

However, there are three particular themes which I want to highlight from this hurried and partial review of the last half-century. The first is the transition from a time of teacher independence to today, when there is much more teacher interdependence. The second is the movement from management to leadership. The third is the shift from LEA control to self-managing and self-governing schools. These three themes might be respectively labelled

- culture

- leadership

- community

and it is to them that I now turn.

Culture

It is very common today to hear school colleagues talking about 'culture'. Usually they refer to their schools' cultures, by which they mean the 'way they do things here'; that is, a set of norms about ways of behaving, perceiving and understanding, underpinned by jointly held beliefs and values. I have been interested in school culture for many years. The school-based research Jennifer Nias and I did with Robin Yeomans and Penny Campbell (Nias *et al.*, 1989,, 1992) helped to develop a number of ideas and insights. Perhaps the most notable of these was the notion of a 'culture of collaboration' (Nias *et al.*, 1989). This organisational culture was one which enabled staff in schools to work closely together and rested on four interacting beliefs: first, individuals should be valued; second, because individuals are inseparable from the groups of which they are a part, groups too should be fostered and valued; third and fourth, the most effective way of promoting these values is by developing a sense of mutual security and openness (Nias *et al.*, 1992: 2).

I have gone back to the original definition of a collaborative culture because in recent years not only has it become popular, but it has also been adopted and translated in a number of different ways. Sometimes it has been used to develop the argument that teachers must work together. Advocates of 'whole school' policies, plans and practices, concerned that there need to be high levels of consistency and continuity among teachers, occasionally emphasise collaboration and ignore what our research said about individuality. I too believe in a measure of consistency among teachers, but regard this as creating unity not uniformity. Collaboration is not something that seeks to clone staff; it is about individuals becoming members of a combined teaching unit while retaining their sense of self. As a combined teaching unit their efforts become more than the sum of their parts and the children benefit accordingly because the staff are building on what colleagues and pupils have previously achieved.

As the foregoing implies, culture has usually been interpreted in terms of teacher cultures. Much important work has gone on here, particularly by Andy Hargreaves (Hargreaves, 1994; Fullan and Hargreaves, 1992). However, what this emphasis on teacher culture highlights is that too little attention has been paid to staff and to pupil cultures in school.

We studied staff cultures in our research into staff relationships in the primary schools (Nias *et al.*, 1989) since we examined how care-takers, secretaries and support staff worked with teachers. Since then there have been a number of significant developments, most notably the introduction of LMS, which have influenced the work of school office staff, and there has been a large increase in the number of classroom assistants. Today almost every class teacher has at least one assistant working alongside him or her for part of every week.

While teachers today may still work apart from other teachers they are no longer isolated from other adults. We urgently need to con-centrate on the roles and development needs of learning-support staff and we need to study how they work effectively with and along-side teachers.

However, perhaps the greatest cultural issue is that of investigating pupil cultures in primary schools. There have been some excellent studies in this area (e.g. Pollard, 1985) but these are now dated. Yet, when teachers talk to me about their classrooms and 'children today', it seems that many perceive primary school pupils as having changed. For example, teachers often mention pupils' concentration spans or describe how children today are relating to one another in different ways than previously. In turn, these points suggest that we may need to look again at childhood to discern whether there are significant changes taking place.

More specifically, there is a good case for trying to find out what pupils think of their schools and of teaching and learning within them. Work in this sphere by Rudduck (1996) in secondary schools offers one line of enquiry, as does the research of Pollard and others (Pollard *et al.*, 1997). In a recent school improvement project in which I have been involved, we systematically collected pupil perception data from group interviews with children in years four and six and found that their views challenged teachers' assumptions about schooling (see Fielding *et al.*, 1999).

Our experience in the Essex Primary School Improvement programme (Southworth and Lincoln, 1999) showed that there are many reasons for taking pupils' views seriously. For one thing, pupils' views can play a major part in improving schools. For another, we found that the pupil data proved to be immensely powerful, perhaps the most powerful agent of change within a sophisticated school improvement strategy. Furthermore, the research team (which consisted of academic and senior LEA staff) acknowledged the enormous potential, not just to enhance school effectiveness, but, at least in some cases, to lead to much more fundamental transformations in schooling. As Fielding and his associates (1999) explain, there were signs in some of the participating schools that children were questioning 'how things are' in their schools and providing alternative interpretations and prescriptions:

There was also some evidence that teachers were prepared to tentatively yet authentically face what Pollard *et al.* (1997) call 'perhaps the biggest challenge of all', namely to 'allow children a share of the power we, as adults, have in their classrooms and lives' (Ibid). (Fielding *et al.*, 1999: 118)

Fielding *et al.*'s analysis of pupil data and its use in schools suggests that teachers were learning about children's perspectives and sometimes acting on behalf of their pupils and working with them. This third category of engagement with pupil data was much more rare than the other two, yet it may be one which offers considerable opportunities for school improvement since it moves from raising teachers' awareness of pupils' views, and advocacy for them, to pupils and teachers as active partners in the educational process, with children becoming co-agents of change (Fielding *et al.*, 1999: 118-20).

Undoubtedly there is more to examine and explore in this domain. School leaders certainly need to consider, from time to time, the relationship between staff culture and the pupil culture in their schools. Are the two in harmony? Are they at odds with one another? In my experience, many teachers believe that when they work effectively with pupils, this has a bearing on how pupils relate to one another. Yet, in truth, this assumption has never been systematically examined. Instead, managers have been fascinated by teacher cultures, because these may have important implications for staff relations, for the micro-politics of the staff room and for how to manage decision-making. I too believe management is concerned with school culture, but also believe this should not continue to be a monocular view, but become a binocular perspective encapsulating both staff and pupil cultures.

For example, given all the emphasis on improving schools it would be very timely to consider whether pupils in high-performing primary schools, or rapidly improving ones, have specific outlooks and perspectives which enhance their schools' ethos. Is there a sense of a pupil 'culture of achievement', which some Ofsted inspectors believe exists when they describe to me the features they associate with successful schools (see Loose, 1997)?

There is also a case for teachers themselves researching, perhaps in association with a local university, the significance of school councils and 'circle time' to the children who participate in them. Similarly, it would be interesting to know what pupil involvement in target-setting looks like to the children. Primary pupils' perspectives on their schools and classrooms are urgently needed to supplement the predominantly teacher and adult viewpoints we presently have. Unless and until we have this knowledge we will only have a very partial perception of primary schooling and of the culture of schools at the close of the century.

Leadership

It is broadly accepted that school leadership matters. Yet primary school leadership is narrowly defined because it is largely understood to mean headship. This has been an enduring feature of school management and leadership thinking. Moreover, not only is the scope of leadership circumscribed by this strong association with headship, but it is also limited by the continuing emphasis on 'heroic' headteachers.

Heroic leadership best describes the way policy-makers regard headship. Of course, headteachers can and do make a difference. One of the reasons individuals choose to become heads is because they know the position offers them the best prospect for influencing the direction of a school. In my work on primary school leadership I have long acknowledged that primary heads are central and pivotal players in the schools they lead (Southworth, 1987, 1995, 1998). They are powerful figures who can directly influence what does and does not happen in 'their' schools. However, this does not mean that they should all, or always, restrict leadership to themselves. In some circumstances, delegation and staff participation can be unwise. But such circumstances are relatively uncommon. In my experience staff welcome being consulted, participating in decision-making and being given opportunities to lead.

Headteachers therefore must try to balance being in control of the school with sharing some of their influence and responsibilities with colleagues. Primary schools, particularly small and medium-sized ones, are, at best, places characterised by teamwork. They are collaborative places where staff purposefully interact and share responsibilities. They are places where many staff lead – deputies, or as I prefer assistant heads, key stage leaders, subject leaders and SENCOs. They have staff groups where membership and leadership are interchangeable. At one time you will take a lead, later you will follow someone else's lead. In these situations leadership is an inclusive process and the property of the group. In effect, there is a leadership exchange constantly taking place. The headteacher's role in these circumstances is to provide leadership opportunities for all, to develop leaders and to orchestrate who leads and when.

Such patterns also mean that staff members are not dependent on one person because leadership is plural not singular. The great difficulty with heroic leadership is that it is lone leadership and thus everyone else in the school becomes reliant on the head. This can mean that we might only be as good as our leader, but will never transcend her or his approach because their conventions create a ceiling to what we might achieve.

Therefore it is encouraging, at long last, to see in the recent green paper technical document (DfEE, 1999) attention being paid to 'leadership groups': '...As schools use more managerial flexibility to cope with the range of new demands being made of them, school leadership is becoming broader than just the headteacher' (DfEE, 1999, para. 75: 24). While this notion needs more detailed explanation, the principle of shared leadership being promoted by central government is very welcome. It is especially welcome news for those assistant heads who do not wish to become headteachers but nevertheless want to play a full part in the school. Hopefully, the idea of a leadership group will enable all deputies and assistant heads to play a fuller role in leading their schools than is sometimes the case at present. Deputies are not individuals waiting to become heads, either in another school or when the head is absent; they are already headteachers, albeit assistant heads. What such a formulation means is that it is headship which must be shared, rather than the deputy's duties fitted around what the head does.

While the future for shared leadership is looking brighter, it nevertheless needs to be accompanied by rather less emphasis on heroic headteachers. Recent moves in medium and larger schools to senior management teams (SMT) may prove to be an appropriate way of developing leadership teams. Wallace and Huckman's (1999) research offers some valuable insights into the workings of these teams although they also caution colleagues about thinking of them as 'dream teams'!

Community

The concept of community has been applied to schools in two senses: in terms of the school as a community; and the school in the community. Here I want to briefly focus on the latter.

Schools today are generally more open to governors and parents. External relations have developed considerably during the last 20 years. In particular, home-school communications have become more active and interactive than formerly. Staff in schools today recognise that links with parents, local agencies and schools are vital to the pupils' well-being and development. Headteachers and others foster and manage these relationships with great care and diligence.

Furthermore, primary schools have long played an important role in the locations where they are situated. Village primary schools are typically portrayed as community centres which act as magnets for parish, church and residents' events. Suburban and urban schools often perform similar roles. Indeed, most schools I know have some kind of community involvement such as musical and sports activities and charity events. What I will now argue for is intended to complement these existing activities.

Primary schools may today be uniquely placed to provide community links and liaison. I do not mean by this that staff somehow become embroiled in extensive social engineering in their localities. Rather, I believe staff in school should establish, sustain and develop links with their communities which are to the advantage of the pupils and their learning.

Schools already draw-in governors, parents and others who can offer children a range of educational activities. At the same time, there is a growing case for schools involving citizens of the third age whose maturity and knowledge may well enable them to take an interest in pupils who are experiencing learning difficulties or who would benefit from having an adult friend to mentor them and take an interest in their school work. The 'early retired' may constitute an enormous pool of untapped talent which might be organised to provide specific, individual help for children.

Furthermore, in addition to these adults playing a supporting role to schools and children's learning, there are many opportunities for these senior citizens to continue their own learning. One headteacher I know who is committed to lifelong learning has established ICT classes in school for members of the community to attend. The children show the adults what the latest technology can do and, importantly, the children teach the adults how to use it. Given that one of the best ways to learn something is to have to teach the skill to someone else, this seems to me to be an excellent way of enhancing pupils' learning as well as being a practical and important symbol of lifelong learning.

Similarly, students may have a role to play. University students can offer significant role models to underachieving children. Through contacts arranged with colleges and universities mutually beneficial opportunities may be established. The idea of a Children's University, as developed in Birmingham, is one innovation which offers scope for adoption elsewhere. Also, programmes of work experience involving secondary and primary schools have long provided older pupils with the chance to take some responsibility for younger ones. Perhaps more of these kinds of contact could be developed.

Schools are usually organised around age cohorts of children – years R to 6, although schools with less than one class per year group have to have mixed-age classes. Where children are organised into age groups it means that during formal teaching and learning sessions they are working alongside their peers, but not interacting with older or younger children. Some schools provide opportunities for older pupils to read to younger ones, or for younger ones to work alongside much older children. Obviously the opportunities for such interaction are greater in primary schools than in separate junior and infant ones. The need to consider transcending the 'ageist structures' of schools seems to me to be something well worth considering. Who knows, in the future we may return to all-age schools catering for, say, 3-14 and key stages 1, 2 and 3 pupils?

At the same time as pupils in school become more globally aware, through the Internet and ICT, there is a counter-case for them also becoming aware of their local environments and what these have to offer in terms of history, geography, culture and local service. Citizenship has belatedly come back into focus recently, although in many, many schools it never went away. Now may be a time when primary school pupils are further encouraged to become active, local citizens. Such moves might also increase local authorities' and elected members' awareness of young children and provide a basis for giving the children greater attention and a louder voice than at present. If pupil involvement is a 'good thing' in schools and if schools begin to take pupils' perspectives seriously then so too should the local community. Learning about democracy should mean that young children learn about local democracy. Children's parliaments and councils are now used in many countries and in some areas of the UK, and these may become more common.

In other words, schools of today and tomorrow need to be both inside and outside focused. Effective schools need to be seen as not only those which enhance pupils' learning achievements and progress in academic subjects, but also as enriching and extending children's social and personal development through planned programmes which draw upon and draw in members of the local community.

Of course, teachers already have enough to manage; so for schools to do more, others will need to become involved. Nor should such provision be a burden on senior staff. Governors, in consultation with the head, might manage such links and put in place a range of activities. Or, if the government is serious about citizenship, 'local community education officers' might need to be appointed for groups of schools. Clearly there are practical problems to overcome, but at this stage these should not detract from the principal of community involvement in primary education and schooling.

Conclusions

These ideas point towards primary schools becoming communities of pupils, staff and leaders who see themselves as members of the local community, drawing on the resources and talents which reside there to provide rich learning programmes for the pupils.

The concept of community, which I have sketched out, is one which moves us away from thinking about schools as organisations. Organisational thinking looks back to industrial and hierarchical structures, implies a mechanistic approach to management and embodies the old assumptions of the factory system. In their architecture and in their internal organisation some schools still reflect factory methods and assumptions about management, which may be why the 'production' metaphor with its language of targets, products and delivery is applied to schools. However, such assumptions offer little help for thinking about managing schools in the future.

Schools of the future need to be managed as inclusive, organic and human places which acknowledge everyone's contribution and achievement. They should be inclusive of children, parents, staff and the community. They will be organic because their organisational structures and processes are flexible and fluid, with staff inter-changing roles and with leadership and followership moving around the group. They should be human, person-centred places which respect individuals' contributions and recognise and value what they can do and are achieving in academic, social and moral dimensions of their learning and lives.

Of course, some schools are already doing much of this, as I have occasionally tried to show. What these examples demonstrate is that, as with many other things, I learned these things from working and looking inside primary schools.

References

Department of Education and Employment (1998) Teachers: meeting the challenge of change DfEE

Department of Education and Employment (1999) Teachers meeting the challenge of change: technical consultation document on pay and performance management DfEE

Ministry of Education (1959) Primary Education London: Her Majesty's Stationery Office

Fielding M., Fuller A. and Loose T. (1999) 'Taking Pupil Perspectives Seriously: the central place of pupil voice in primary school improvement' in Southworth G. and Lincoln P. (eds.) Understanding Improving Primary schools: Insights and findings from the Essex Primary School Improvement Programme London: Falmer

Fullan M. and Hargreaves A. (1992) What's worth Fighting for in Your School? Buckingham: Open University Press

Hargreaves A. (1994) Changing Teachers, Changing Times London: Cassell

Loose T. (1997) 'Achievement Culture' Managing Schools Today May

Nias J., Southworth G. and Yeomans R. (1989) Staff Relationships in the Primary School: A study of organisational cultures London: Falmer

Pollard A. (1985) The Social World of the Primary School London: Cassell

Pollard A., Thiessen D. and Filer A. (eds.) (1996) Children and Their Curriculum London: Falmer

Rudduck J., Chaplain R. and Wallace G. (eds.) (1996) School Improvement: What can pupils tell us? London: Fulton

Southworth G. (1987) 'Primary School Headship and Collegiality' in Southworth G.(ed.) Readings in Primary School Management London: Falmer

Southworth G. (1995) Looking Into Primary Headship: A research based interpretation London: Falmer

Southworth G. (1998) Leading Improving Primary Schools: the work of heads and deputy headteachers London: Falmer

Southworth G. and Lincoln P. (eds.) (1999) Supporting Improving Primary Schools: The role of heads and LEAs in raising standards London: Falmer

Wallace M. and Huckman L. (1999) Senior Management Teams in Primary Schools London: Routledge

TEACHER PROFESSIONAL DEVELOPMENT AND THE SOUND OF A HANDCLAP

Marion Dadds

Octber 1971. My probationary class is just hovering on the boundary between control and disintegration. Five different group activities are in full swing, the way we were taught at college. Enthusiasm is spiralling upwards into disruption. Paper, scissors and a loosely identified autonomy prevail. This is just the kind of time you don't want the head to enter. But enter he does. I clap my hands for some order as he leans towards me, the better to hear my ailing voice. My pathetic handclap diminishes into a puff of wind.

My one and only probationary professional development event follows. The head cups his large hands into large globes. He brings them together smartly. The swift impact produces a deafening two-hand clap. The children stop, stunned, in their tracks. Then, in full view of my astonished class, the head insists I practise my way through this handclap routine step by step. At the sixth attempt I produce the necessary explosion at a volume to satisfy his sense of quality and standard. The children spontaneously beginning to clap and cheer, only to be as spontaneously silenced by his withering glare. For the first time in two months, since I started this difficult and dangerous career with them, the children continue their work in a hushed aura. My supported professional development for the year is over.

Like most probationary, newly qualified teachers at that time, I struggled on for the rest of the year alone, drawing from whatever impromptu listening ears I could muster from friends and colleagues. There was much joy and success in this first year of my career but the experience was also, at times, isolating and fragmented. Extended conversations in which I might have been better able to process, and come to understand, my work were not part of this experience though they were central to my need. I longed to share the complexity and difficulty of my work with mature professionals who could help me to gain a broader perspective on the many new practical and intellectual challenges facing me daily. A competent mentor, willing to listen to my many questions and offer advice, would have been a luxury. How should I teach reading, discipline, self-confidence, independence, social skills? How could I best prepare for an art lesson, a city visit? How ought I to teach mathematical concepts and skills that seemed a mystery to the young minds over which I had substantial power and control? How could I hear all the children read daily? Did I need to, and why? How might I work with, and relate effectively to, the children's families? And how could I do all this with patience, sympathy and encouragement in a way that would allow my pupils to feel well of themselves as learners, questioners, social beings, at a time when I was clinging tightly to my own learning curve? Unfortunately, I was not given access to any of the expertise I needed to make sense of such questions in this crucial formative year.

There were also philosophical uncertainties to confront. Where, for example, was the justice, in this city context, of a common education for children with a less than common social, educational and material endowment; where the most fortunate child in my class spent her Christmas holidays ski-ing with her family whilst the least fortunate resorted to stealing others' presents, having received none themselves? Some mothers spent a good deal of their time in the fashion department in John Lewis's whilst others worked both day and night shifts, fetching, carrying, cleaning in local hospitals, surgeries and the homes of those out shopping at John Lewis's. Where did Rousseau's views of what was appropriate for Emile fit into these circumstances, I wondered? How did the client-centred attitudes of Carl Rogers (1961), with his notion of unconditional positive regard, to which I was deeply committed, speak to the challenges I faced as I had to deal with the Christmas thefts by the most deprived and disturbed children in my class? I wanted the educational theories I had met at college in the 1960s to serve my thinking and practice in a way that ensured I did not fall into the trap of theoretical cynicism. But I was unsure how they could. There were deep-seated questions, therefore, which I could not answer in a dilemma-free way as a lone teacher, but they were questions that haunted me daily as I took upon myself the impossible burden of trying to compensate these children for what society would never offer them. I often felt morally lost in these open plains of social disadvantage, recognising my prime duty to offer a structured education for my pupils whilst upholding the moral simplicities of the school; moral simplicities that served, in many ways, to sustain the unjust social order. I rarely felt well enough equipped with all the knowledge, skills and emotional fortitude to understand, let alone administer, the many facets of this professional challenge.

Had I been able to write my own professional development programme at that time, it would have been wide ranging and demanding. It would have embraced the need for the growth of myriad practical classroom skills; the development of curriculum knowledge into areas which lay beyond my own specialism in the language arts (I never did feel, for example, that I mastered what was required to give my pupils a good art education, having failed badly myself in school). A self-invented development programme would have given me access to talk and debate with other teachers in which I might have been able to shape my own views and judgements more coherently. There would have been time to re-read some of the influential writers I'd come across in my training and to discuss with others how these could be related to the practical world of the classroom with my 43 pupils. Time would have been available to visit experienced teachers, to observe and discuss their practice, their philosophies, their ways of interacting with children, their approaches to planning and organisation. My ideal professional development programme would have helped to educate further my ideas, ideals, feelings, attitudes and classroom practices. I would also have welcomed thousands of 'tips for teachers' to help put practical flesh on my ideas and ideals, for I knew primary teaching to be, without doubt, located in a practical culture in which professionals like myself enjoyed the 'doing' of our work as much as intellectualising it. I have never been able to support the false polarisation often made between reflective, intellectual professional development and the less reflective 'tips-for-teachers' approach. Both were beneficial in different ways and should have been married rather than separated. The satisfaction in teaching came from successful action that inspired and motivated children to achieve what they had not achieved before. In this sense, practice is ideological, just as ideology is emotional for it is in these realisations for children that teaching moves and motivates us.

Times have changed, of course, in the three decades since I mastered the technique of the two hand clap. We now understand better the value of professional talk and observation in shaping teachers' ideas and practices (Smyth, 1991). We understand more about the importance of professional communities and social learning which tend towards cultures of collaboration (Nias *et al.*, 1989, Lieberman and Miller, 1991). Much has been learned of the benevolent impact that thoughtful classroom action research can have on teachers' growth (eg. Dadds, 1995, Holly, 1991). Research has taught us about the inexorable influence of the teacher's own biography (Goodson 1992) and personal theories drawn from thoughtful reflections on experience (o' Hanlon, 1993). We understand more about the part that good partnership arrangements with schools and Local Education Authorities can have (James, 1994) and the need for sustained professional development, rather than short, isolated experiences, if learning is to be effective (Morley, 1994). There is also evidence that sound professional development requires of the teacher a sense of courage and tenacity, for learning of this order involves significant personal transformation, often of a highly turbulent, emotional and self-exposing kind (Hollingsworth, 1994, Drummond and McLaughlin, 1994, Dadds, 1994). For this, safe learning climates are essential: hostility, authoritarianism and excessive negative feedback are dysfunctional (Bradley *et al*, 1989).

We have also come to value teacher professional development more clearly than before – and to offer a wider range of structured opportunities, using the resources inside school as well as drawing expertise from outside (Lee, 1997, Morley, 1994). Teachers have been able to profit from a variety of provision, though support has often been patchy and inconsistent in different parts of the country (Lee, 1997). The rise, fall and re-structuring of teachers' centres, for example, enabled teachers and their representatives to define, and provide for, their own perceived needs (Gough, 1997). The short, practical courses which teachers' centres offered could liberate the uninitiated into new-found classroom competence. For example, the six-session course which I attended on playing the guitar at the local teachers' centre in my fourth teaching year, had a benign effect on my classroom practice, my pupils and their regard for me as a human being. This new skill added to my status in the eyes of children and parents. It added to my own self-image as I mastered what I thought I never would. And it enhanced the daily ethos I tried to create. Music became an integral part of our lives. It lifted us when we were down; soothed us when we were fractured; bound us more closely when we were at odds. It also encouraged children to produce their own music and songs in a way I could not have predicted. My evolving understanding of music education was realised, therefore, in the application of practice. Professional development often has this serendipitous quality.

Universities and other higher education institutions have had their continuing part to play, too. Here, on certificate, diploma and master's courses, teachers have been offered the intellectual space in which to conceptualise their work more broadly than the confines of their schools and classrooms often allow. Here, the professional mind can be developed to deeper levels (Greene, 1973). This intellectual and theoretical form of professional development can, of course, be isolating in some schools (Dadds, 1986). In one staff meeting I attended as a young teacher, for example, a colleague who was attending a master's course at the local university, and who dared to refer to some relevant theory he had been reading on children's learning, was scorned for his 'airy-fairy theory' by a member of senior management. He was accused of 'thinking too much', an

127

accusation which devastated him for some time to come. The colleague, who had much to offer, never again referred to his master's learning in the staffroom. Thus, his own development was never valued by the institution and was never drawn upon as a resource for the rest of us in the school. Cynical cultures can inhibit their own growth and that of their members. In contrast, in a school where I was later in my life to do research on research-based professional development (Dadds, 1995), senior management had thoughtful, well-managed strategies for using the developmental capital of staff to enrich school development and improve children's learning experiences. There was an established tradition of advanced professional development in this school which went back years. Here, colleagues in general felt good about their learning. It was not a part of their lives which they felt compelled to hide. For them, sharing the fruits of their in-service work was second nature; an expectation; an integral part of the learning culture; a cultural norm.

Into this framework of growing opportunities, developmental teacher appraisal stepped in 1991. This was an attempt, based on evaluated pilot studies, to bring development and accountability together in a way that enabled teachers and schools to maintain control over their growth whilst acknowledging their responsibilities to keep pace with the rapidly changing social and educational context.

Developmental appraisal was the first structured, national effort to seek a balance between the desires of individual teachers and the directions in which the school as a whole was trying to move. In the early stages of my teaching career, we did our own thing when we signed up for courses. Funding came from outside the school, usually from Local Education Authorities, so there was no in-school gate-keeping. Professional development was a personal affair. When developmental appraisal appeared on the scene, those days of individualism were passing rapidly. The change agenda was being set from the centre by virtue of the content of educational reform: curriculum, assessment, testing, special needs, management came to the fore, impacting on school development plans and, by implication, on the professional development plans of individual teachers. Funds were delegated to schools: monetary gate-keeping came into operation. Dilemmas often arose between investing in in-service courses that matched the school development agenda and those which matched the perceived interests of individual teachers. Attending a course on tapestry and weaving, for example, would not be seen as a priority in a school suffering severe literacy problems. This raised tensions for some between school and self which developmental appraisal could not always resolve satisfactorily. Some teachers started paying for their own courses when they felt passionately the need to pursue interests that lay outside the school agenda and the scope of the budget. Many still do.

Despite the increasing grip of the centralist agenda, many teachers and headteachers welcomed the new opportunity that developmental appraisal offered to hold regular discussions of classroom practice based on collected evidence (Bradley *et al*, 1989). Here was a new emphasis on, and analysis of, each teacher's classroom practice. Where the system worked well, dialogue, self-analysis, peer observation, reflection, evidence and critique served teachers' learning positively. A climate of trust, support and mutual respect seemed crucial to such success. Socially-based learning, especially that between managers and managed, needs openness and honesty and, by implication, will only flourish in psychologically safe places (Dadds, 1990). In some schools where these conditions did not prevail, developmental appraisal was less successful (Bartlett, 1998). By many, unfortunately, it is still seen as one more bureaucratic expectation that does little, if anything, to enhance status, working practices and resources; a process in which teachers expose their developmental needs in a way that may, subsequently, be used against them (Bradley *et al*, 1989). Thus, some school cultures have been unable to exploit the potential of this form of appraisal.

One major outcome of appraisal, however, was to establish professional development as both an entitlement and an expectation. This has fostered a national climate in which continuous learning is seen as an essential part of one's role as a teacher. With the constant rapid changes in society and in government demands, this is necessary. The growth of technology, for example, as one aspect of momentous change, has frightened and de-skilled many. The technological revolution is affecting our children's lives and futures at unprecedented rates: it is a revolution in which children's knowledge is often in advance of that of their teachers. New attitudes and teaching methods are needed to adapt to these circumstances. So new forms of supported professional development are essential to promote the learning which many teachers need in order to keep pace and extend their practices.

Yet such rapid changes have led, for many, to change overload, stress and, in severe cases, burn-out (Hargreaves, 1998, Nias, 1991). Too much imposed professional learning, too fast, can be dangerous, achieving the opposite of what we might desire, especially in our national climate of derision which has, on the whole, imaged teachers negatively. A professional willingness to improve can, thus, be overtaken by a resentment at too much centralist enforcement at too rapid a pace (Dadds, 1998). This, sadly, has been the case for many, leading to withdrawal from the profession of good and dedicated teachers. And, of course, the move away from developmental appraisal towards performance-related pay (Carvel, 1999:13) might strip the more effective schools of benign and effective collaborative processes that contribute to the growth of professional skill, understanding and confidence. This may lead to a further erosion of developmental potential from the profession.

This inexorable shift of control from the teacher to the state has heralded a marked shift in notions of professionalism as we have moved from autonomy into imposition and coercion. This, in turn, is affecting views of what professional development might mean, as support for teacher and school change is now focused solely on the government's change agenda. In this climate, professional training, rather than development, has become the dominant change methodology and mode of provision for teachers' learning. The government has made it clear that there is no room for individual preferences in professional development that lie outside the national direction (and note the confusion between training and development):

> Much existing training is unsystematic and unfocused. We intend to set out a clear framework for professional development which brings together national, school and individual training priorities to help all teachers to raise standards in the classroom ... (DfEE, 1998: 48).

All national training programmes for educational reform since 1998 have been designed to fulfil this same purpose of delivering the central agenda. I have attended several training events over the years for implementation of the national curriculum, assessment and testing, governor training and the literacy hour. As professional experiences, they are significantly different in character from in-service development, emphasising information, skills and practices at the expense of understanding and critical appraisal. As educative events, therefore, they leave much to be desired. They have tended to be non-reflective, non-argumentative, non-intellectualised, withholding opportunities for teachers to bring their own judgements to bear on pedagogy, curricula and the innovations they have been asked to implement (Dadds, 1998). In the process, the programmes have intellectually de-skilled many experienced teachers, causing them to question the validity of their professional judgement and leading to a sense of insecurity about their practice. In this sense, reflective-free training can be professionally dysfunctional.

The national training frameworks for curricula, assessment and testing, of course, have the advantage of offering an entitlement to children as well as guidance for teachers and headteachers. The details of professional development programmes are not left so much to chance as before. But they carry the acute disadvantage of wresting power, control and ownership from the professionals themselves. Others have noted that this is contributing to de-professionalisation of the teaching force (eg. Richards, 1999, Hargreaves, 1998). This 'do-as-you're-told' or obedience model flies in the face of a good deal of evidence on teacher thinking which suggests that professional development is most effective when schools and teachers have control and ownership over their own development programmes and processes (Clark, 1992, Jackson, 1992, Webb, 1998).

Despite this shift of power from periphery to centre, the key questions for professional development remain the same as they were in my early years of teaching. What kind of teachers do we want for our children and how will we support them in their professional growth towards those ends? There are different and competing views of what it means to be an educator but it seems self-evident that we will always want teachers who are kind, respectful, knowledgeable, empathetic, committed to social justice. It also seems self-evident that to be an educator, one has to be educated oneself, rather than merely trained. So we also want forms of professional development that encourage teachers to have informed minds of their own; to ask critical questions of themselves, education and society; to develop beliefs and values which are shaped through thoughtful reflection on experience rather than imposed authority; to develop as responsible, free-minded professionals. Without these qualities, a teacher may have little to offer to the intellectual development of children growing up in a supposedly free and democratic society.

So what of the future? Like many others, I hope that we can move forward in education with a new view of professional development that takes us beyond both the unstructured, 'do-as-you-like' individualism of my early teaching years and the centralist 'do-as-you're-told' approach of today. In this, it is hoped that we will be able to embed a freely adopted sense of responsibility for our own professional growth into the culture of teaching generally, despite government plans to make such a commitment a contractual obligation (DfEE, 1998). Such a voluntary attitude to professional development would not be insular nor egocentric but would be responsive to societal needs. It would also recognise the need for the growth of teachers' critical intellect as well as their classroom practices.

If such responsible critical autonomy, through the creation of a General Teaching Council, can replace the power-coercive strategies of government today, as well as fostering collaboration rather than competition, then we may be able to return professional development to the profession with some confidence and optimism.

The capacity for such critical professional autonomy seems essential if our teachers are to continue to make the growing contribution society requires of them, for higher and higher expectations are now being placed on teachers by politicians and communities alike (Stewart and McCann, 1999). Some believe that the role of the teacher must be radically re-thought, or re-envisioned (Graham, 1998, Cranston, 1998) if education is to make a significant contribution to the global changes predicted for the new millennium and to the development of economically healthy nations. 'The expectation is that the breadth and pace of....change will increase such that the demands on teachers.....will require different mind-sets and new skills' (Cranston, 1998: 381). These are exacting demands.

Yet in the UK, we have been living with this contradiction in which 'the horizons of school teachers.... have been narrowed by the curricular prescriptions of the nation state, which has contrived to promote the doctrine of global competitiveness while pursuing the pedagogical politics of cultural isolation' (Graham, 1998: 11). Continuing to bind teachers' thoughts, actions and values in the straitjacket of state edicts will not be helpful if professional judgement, intellect and commitment are to contribute benignly to such rapid social and global change. The latest thoughts from the Department for Education and Employment (DfEE, 2000) on professional development may be helpful here in that there seems finally to be a recognition of the need for teachers to have a sense of ownership over their professional development and to be well supported in this by government and Local Education Authority opportunities. Such ownership, if it is to be educative and professional, will inevitably require acts of critical appraisal, not blind acceptance of the singular views of government.

Indeed, it has been argued (UCET, 1999) that the future of the teaching profession, and education itself, is in jeopardy if we do not move from the narrow, technicist, power-coercive political approach of the past years into one which releases and fosters teachers' creative and intellectual powers for the benefit of wider communities. The teacher which the future needs may not be the teacher of the past so 'we need to think afresh', to re-envision teachers as 'learning professionals' who would act as teachers themselves and also facilitators of others, 'who have things to pass on to those who wish to learn' (ibid:1). Teachers of the future would be lynch-pins at the centre of learning communities. They would acknowledge that learning is a social phenomenon and would work in a variety of ways accordingly in order to champion learning and generate learning networks (ibid).

Such a vision, if relevant and realistic, would be demanding of teachers. The role could not be fulfilled through prescription or unreflective obedience. It would require responsible independence of mind, spirit, judgement and action within a moral framework. Qualities of open-mindedness, empathy, social responsibility and communication would be central. Learning professionals would be critical thinkers, open to new learning themselves, seeing learning as a lifelong enterprise for themselves and others, accepting continuing professional development as natural and essential. The demands on programmes of professional development would be substantial, but the rewards could be well worth the investment. The passing-on of handclapping skills would contribute little.

The immediate future of progress, however, is likely to lie, first and foremost, in the classroom and in the continuing enhancement of pedagogy (DfEE, 2000: 6). The new financial incentives for excellent teachers to stay close to children, rather than pursue the traditional career ladder through the management hierarchy, is designed to contribute to this focus. This, too, brings in its wake many new demands. Exceptional teachers will be required not only to maintain their excellent standard of teaching but also to disseminate good practice and influence others, as will their colleagues in the training schools envisioned by the Labour government (Morris, 1999). Doing this requires teachers to make explicit their theories about teaching and learning, an intellectual process which demands thoughtful, critical reflection and well-developed powers of sensitive communication. In addition, more teachers are now making a significant contribution to the pedagogic education and training of student teachers in new partnership arrangements and school-based training. This demands the development of mentoring capacities, the ability to explain and share good practice with novices, the capacity to judge carefully, evaluate, support, encourage, as well as collaborate with partners in other schools and higher education institutions. In all these aspects of the developing role, classroom teachers are, themselves, more prominently engaged as agents of others' professional development, so new areas of learning are needed to fulfil these roles successfully.

The attempted moves by the Teacher Training Agency towards developing teaching as a research-based profession will, likewise, place new expectations on teachers in a context which is already overloaded with change. If this particular initiative is to have any meaning for the improvement of teaching and learning, new forms of critical 'research literacy' are needed in order to use others' research, as well as learning to do one's own. Critical judgement is required to analyse, interpret and apply research with validity, for evidence about teaching and learning that teachers might want to draw upon is neither neutral nor value-free. Herein lies a further reason for valuing critical professional autonomy of mind in a context in which teachers are expected to make sense of increasing amounts of research and accountability material (Morris, 1999) as a necessary aspect of their work.

I often wonder what that goodly headteacher who taught me the sound of a handclap is doing now. Maybe, if he's still alive, he's basking in a well-earned retirement, free from the exacting responsibilities of so much educational change, for, despite his limitations in supporting the development of his new teachers, he ran a well-ordered, well-disciplined school, characteristic of the times and in difficult circumstances. And whatever the shortcomings in provision were then, both in school and nationally, at least there was more than enough opportunity for me to develop my own views and values; to learn from my own mistakes and successes; to think my own professional thoughts and pursue my own professional judgements in the best way I knew, keeping the children's educational interests as the central reference point, as did the head. More thorough support would have been welcome, I admit. More guiding frameworks for teaching and learning would have provided useful structures in the open plains of teacher freedom. But I would not have been happy to have been a newly qualified teacher in another age which required unreflective obedience to the many authoritarian, centralist handclaps that have been around. Such obedient conformity would not, I believe, have been in the best professional interests of my new qualified peers nor, in the long run, in the best interests of our pupils. We cannot educate children for a free-thinking, rapidly changing society by binding the intellect, practices and judgements of their teachers. An attitude shift is needed from central authorities if teachers are to be adequately supported in the changes ahead and if we are to benefit in the future from the knowledge about professional development we have gained to date. If governments misjudge this for teachers, they also misjudge it for children. If they judge well, children will be the beneficiaries.

Bibliography

Bartlett, S. (1998) 'The development of effective appraisal by teachers' in British Journal of In-service Education, vol. 24, no.2, pp.227-238

Bradley, H. et al. (1989) Evaluation of the school teacher appraisal pilot study, Cambridge Institute of Education, Cambridge

Carvel, J. (1999) 'Plan to shame the coasters' in The Guardian, 6th February

Clark, C. (1992) 'Teachers as designers of self-directed professional development' in Hargreaves, A and Fullan, M.G., eds., 1992, Understanding teacher development, Teachers' College Press, New York

Cranston N.C. (1998) 'Preparing teachers for the new millennium: are we doing enough?' in British Journal of In-service Education, Vol. 24, No. 3, pp. 381-391

Dadds, M. (1986) 'The school, the teacher researcher and the in-service tutor' in Classroom Action Research Network, Vol. 7,pp.96-107

Dadds, M. (1990) Teacher appraisal for teacher development in Cambridge Institute of Education Newsletter, Cambridge, January

Dadds, M. (1994) 'Bridging the gap: using the school-based project to link award-bearing INSET to school development' in Bradley, H et al., eds., 1994, Developing teachers, developing schools, Fulton, London

Dadds, M. (1995) Passionate enquiry and school development: a story about teacher action research, Falmer, London

Dadds, M. (1997) Continuing professional development: nurturing the expert within in British Journal of In-service Education, vol. 23, no.1, pp.31-38

Dadds, M. (1998) 'Some politics of pedagogy' paper presented to the annual conference of the Standing Committee for the Education and Training of Teachers, Rugby

Department for Education and Employment (1998) Teachers meeting the challenge of change, The Stationery Office, London

Department for Education and Employment (2000) Professional development: support for teaching and learning, DfEE, February

Drummond, M.J. and McLaughlin, C. (1994) 'Teaching and learning – the fourth dimension' in Bradley, H et al., eds., 1994, Developing teachers, developing schools, Fulton, London

Gough, B. (1997) 'Teachers' centres as seen through the pages of the British Journal of In-service Education' in British Journal of In-service Education, vol. 23, no. 1, pp.23-30

Goodson, I. (1992) 'Sponsoring the teacher's voice: teachers' lives and teacher development' in Hargreaves, A and Fullan, M.G., eds, 1992, Understanding teacher development, Teachers' College Press, New York

Graham, J. (1998) 'From new right to new deal: nationalism, globalisation and the regulation of teacher professionalism' in British Journal of In-service Education, Vol. 24, No. 1, pp.9-29

Greene, M. (1973) Teacher as stranger, Wadsworth, Belmont

Hargreaves, A. (1998) The emotional politics of teaching and teacher development: with implications for educational leadership, paper presented to the American Educational Research Association Annual Conference, San Diego, April

Hollingsworth, S. (1994) Teacher research and urban literacy education, Teachers College Press, New York

Jackson, P. (1992) 'Helping teachers develop' in Hargreaves, A and Fullan, M.G., eds., 1992, Understanding teacher development, Teachers' College Press, New York

James, M. (1994) 'Local education authority and higher education partnership in support of school-based development projects' in Bradley, H et al., eds, 1994, Developing teachers, developing schools, Fulton, London

Lee, M. (1997) 'The development of in-service education and training as seen through the pages of the British Journal of In-service Education' in British Journal of In-service Education, Vol. 23, No. 1, pp.9-22

Lieberman, A. and Miller, A., eds. (1991) Staff development for education in the '90s, Teachers' College Press, New York

Morley, G. (1994) 'Recent developments in in-service education and training for teachers' in Bradley, H et al., eds., 1994, Developing teachers, developing schools, Fulton, London

Morris, E. (1999) Keynote address to the Universities Council for the Education of Teachers Annual Conference, November

Nias, J. (1991) 'Changing times, changing identities: grieving for a lost self' in Burgess, R., ed., Educational research and evaluation: for policy and practice, Falmer, Lewes

Nias, J., Southworth, G. and Yeomans, R. (1989) Staff relationships in the primary school, Cassell, London

o' Hanlon, C (1993) 'The importance of an articulated personal theory of professional development' in Elliott, J, ed., 1993, Reconstructing teacher education: teacher development, Falmer, London

Richards, C. (1999) 'Teaching as an evidence-based profession', keynote lecture given to the UCET conference, Teaching as an evidence-based profession, Newcastle, February

Rogers, C. (1961) On becoming a person, Constable, London

Smyth, J. (1991) Teachers as collaborative learners, Open University Press, Buckingham

Stewart, D and McCann, P. (1999) 'Educators and the law: implications for the professional development of school administrators and teachers' in British Journal of In-service Education, Vol. 25, No. 1, pp. 135-150

Universities Council for the Education of Teachers (1999) New directions in teacher education and training: some proposals, UCET

Webb, R., Vulliamy, G., Hakkinen, K. and Hamalainenen, S. (1998) External inspection or school self-evaluation? A comparative analysis of policy and practice in primary schools in England and Finland in British Educational Research Journal, Vol. 24, No. 5

CHANGING ASPECTS OF PRIMARY TEACHERS' PROFESSIONALISM:
driving forward or driven backward?

Denis Hayes

Preface

A few years into the twenty-first century, the newly created coalition government makes the following announcement:

Owing to spiralling costs and the failure of primary schools to meet government implementation targets (GITs), plans are in hand to construct a Core Primary School for the whole of the United Kingdom. Existing schools will be retained as satellite components, to be known as Cerebral Units. Multimedia links will provide the necessary communication channels between the Core School and the Units. The school, to be known as the Dome Academy, will be located in the capital. The anticipated date of opening is September 2006. A team of fifty subject specialist teachers, to be known as Dome Professionals, are to be appointed as soon as possible to transmit lessons to the nation. Anyone wishing to apply for a post as Dome Professional must have outstanding subject knowledge, proven teaching ability and the necessary skills to communicate to an audience through distance learning. Remuneration will be based on a scale linked to improvements across national standards in core subjects. For further information contact The Standards Tsar, Dome Place, London WD40 IC2.

Introduction

The above scenario might leave you wondering whether the author has taken leave of his senses or might have touched a nerve about your fears for the future of primary education and the state of the profession. You may have serious doubts about the efficacy of promoting and maintaining a functional curriculum, with high political rewards for any party that can demonstrate that it has succeeded in raising arbitrarily designated standards where others have failed (Farrell, 1999).

In questioning whether the establishment of a computer-interactive Dome Academy with a staff of Dome Professionals is anything other than a flight of fancy, it is worth bearing in mind that the rate of technological advance over the past few years has been astounding. The prospect of a single, centralised school with a network of computer-linked feeder schools is technologically within reach. It could be argued that there is merit in bringing together the very best teachers in a central school to deliver the highest quality lessons in core subjects to the nation's children. If a core curriculum has to be applied consistently, then the introduction of a learning superhighway, operated centrally and monitored locally, has a certain appeal.

On the other hand, you may hesitate at the thought of any moves towards a further centralisation of education provision. Cheap, certainly. Efficiently delivered, perhaps. But your instinct, educational values and desire for a creative, dynamic learning society are opposed to such a highly regulated system. You cannot shake off a deep-seated horror at the prospect of a narrowly based curriculum delivered in packages of knowledge to a widely diverse audience of pupils in different contexts.

At the core of your unease will probably lie serious concerns over the professional status of primary teachers and the prospect that new legislation always seems to result in a further curbing of autonomy, such that teaching becomes 'deprofessionalised or reprofessionalised', despite the rhetoric of professionalism contained in official policy documents (Welch and Mahoney, 2000: 139). If we are to explore the issues associated with the concept of a Dome Professional, it is essential to be clear about what we mean when we use the term 'profession' and its derivative, 'professionalism' (Ozga and Lawn, 1981). We must also consider whether there is anything distinctive about being a professional in a primary phase setting as opposed to any other sphere of education.

Definitions

One of the challenges in handling a term like 'professionalism' is that it can be described in a number of ways:

1. Professionalism as a function of DOING. That is, teachers can demonstrate that they have mastered the skills of effective teaching and ability to motivate children.

2. Professionalism as a function of BEING. That is, teachers can show by their active participation in school life, character, interpersonal skills and cooperative disposition, that they make a significant contribution to the establishment and maintenance of a positive learning climate.

3. Professionalism as a function of KNOWING. That is, teachers have strong subject knowledge and can transfer this into their teaching of children and support for colleagues.

4. Professionalism as a function of COMPLYING. That is, teachers accept and internalise externally imposed directives and translate them into their classroom practice.

5. Professionalism as a function of REDEFINING. That is, teachers take a given set of requirements and adapt, modify, create and manipulate them to suit the particular conditions of the school and classroom.

Although it may be possible to combine some of the above functions, the final two definitions (complying and redefining) appear to be irreconcilable. If teachers' professionalism resides in their ability to comply with government-imposed legislation, a definition of the professional role relates directly to how closely they can, or will, conform to the external requirements. If by professional we mean that teachers develop insights into the way that children learn best in a variety of contexts, and redefine their approach accordingly, we are looking at a definition that extends well beyond a technicist, compliant mode. Of course, primary teachers may attempt to satisfy both criteria by outwardly complying but at the same time subtly subverting and refining the standard specification to make it 'fit' their situation. Those who object to being coerced into teaching particular things in a particular way may justify their opposition on the basis that an over-regulated system prevents them from making the fine judgements about what is appropriate for their pupils in their classroom in their school (Dann and Simco, 2000). Those who enjoy the benefits of being told what to do and when to do it will consider that a strong component of their professionalism is to 'make things work' rather than complaining about an imperfect situation. For many primary teachers, a definition of professionalism based on their ability to achieve higher test results, while marginalising their judgements about pupils' capability, relegating relationships to the status of an outmoded sentimentalism and giving short thrift to altruism and self-sacrifice as a motivation for teaching, may be viewed as negating the very professionalism it purports to serve.

The changing nature of professional autonomy

At the heart of the argument about a valid definition of professionalism lies the issue of teacher autonomy. In the years following the publication of the Plowden report (CACE, 1967) primary teachers and educators were generally optimistic about the future. Primary teachers were not unduly constrained by externally imposed regulations, and within schools there was considerable variation in the extent to which teachers controlled what was taught and the way it was done. Interest in primary education was largely apolitical, contrasting sharply with the stormy debate raging over the future of secondary schooling during the same period. Teachers were not used to having their practice challenged, other than by occasional visits from Her Majesty's Inspectors (HMI) and Local Education Authority advisers.

Despite the apparent tranquillity, however, some of the less publicised aspects of the Plowden report were already trickling into the minds of policy makers, including proposals that would, some ten or fifteen years later, form the basis for significant reforms and impact fiercely on teachers' professionalism. For instance, specialised teaching towards the top end of the primary school, formal inspections, parental choice of school and action to improve less popular schools, were all mentioned in the Plowden report (see Benford, 1998). Unfortunately, teachers in the late 1960s and 1970s were not always willing or able to present a clear rationale for their teaching, a shortcoming that was to disadvantage them when the debate about the purpose of education became more intense. On the occasions when criticisms were levelled about the state of education, then 'misguided and inappropriately defensive arguments were put forward by primary teachers that they taught children not subjects of the curriculum' (Norris, 1995: 95). Sweetman notes that 'against this busy political front, the centralisation of the curriculum continued quietly with both the Department of Education and Science (DES) and HMI suggesting ways in which a common school curriculum might develop' (Sweetman, 1992: 8).

The Ruskin College speech (October, 1976) by the then Labour Prime Minister, James Callaghan, in which he expressed concern about the use of informal methods of teaching, low standards of numeracy in school and the importance of getting value for money, catapulted education into the political arena. His intervention signalled the beginning of the end of teachers' freedom to organise their work according to their personal disposition; instead, all eyes were turning to ways in which pupils in all schools might be equipped for the world of the twenty-first century (DES/Welsh Office, 1985, 1992). Questions were raised about the teaching methods used by primary teachers, the variable standards of reading, writing and arithmetic that existed across the country, and the widely differing school curricula. Primary teachers' professionalism was generally perceived as containing a strong element of 'childminding'. Consequently, the widely held belief that 'anyone can do it' crept into the public psyche about teaching. Considerable industrial unrest in the late 1960s and 1970s added to the perception that teachers were merely pseudo-intellectuals with too much time on their hands.

Other changes were intruding on the professional autonomy that primary teachers had enjoyed for so long. For instance, until the

1980s, the use of timetables and subject headings in primary education was largely restricted to the private sector. The word 'lesson' was seen as applying only to secondary school teaching. Many primary teachers were uneasy at the prospect of having to plan lessons to fit a time-frame, believing that such restrictions were artificial and did not take account of the differing rates at which children learned and the complex nature of the process. Nevertheless, the publication of studies and reports in the late 1980s and early 1990s cast doubt on some deeply rooted aspects of professional practice, especially the role of the primary teacher as 'facilitating' children's learning, rather than actively teaching. Significantly, the discussion paper by Alexander *et al.* (1992), written in response to the then Secretary of State's desire to review available evidence about the delivery of education in primary schools, and the follow-up report by Ofsted (1993), suggested that more emphasis on whole-class teaching and single-subject lessons would enhance children's learning. At the same time, the soothing terminology of 'infant and 'junior', indicators of the civilising role of teachers, was replaced by more impersonal language (key stages 1 and 2), together with an increasing emphasis upon structure, continuity, progression and the new buzzword 'accountability' (see Poulson, 1998). Well-worn expressions such as 'child-centred' and 'nurturing' were overrun by marketplace terminology: objectives, outcomes, monitoring, performance.

As primary practitioners' autonomy weakened, the concept of teachers as the sole educators of children was being replaced by an acknowledgement that as learning begins at home, partnership in learning between school and home is an essential feature of effective education. The Parents' Charter (DES, 1991) helped to transform the parents' role from one of interested bystander to an amalgam of client, partner and consumer. The professional bedrock of primary teachers that they knew what was best for the children ('Trust me, I'm a teacher') was overtaken by the new phenomenon of primary teachers being challenged over their opinion of what was best and having to justify it to the watching world of parents, governors and (increasingly) the newly created Ofsted inspectorate.

Disappointed hopes

In the space of a few years, primary teachers' freedom to determine their own and their pupils' destiny had been overtaken by a centrally controlled education system dominated by principles of consumerism and performance. The type of professionalism emerging during the 1980s and 1990s made many formal demands on teachers, including demonstrable mastery of subject-specific knowledge, an ability to establish clearly defined learning objectives in advance of lessons, the need to assess accurately pupils' progress and achievement, and the implementation of a rigid and heavily prescribed national curriculum (Troman, 1996). Events moved at a rapid pace, leaving primary teachers breathless and leading to well-founded complaints of information overload. A new expression, 'teacher burn-out' entered the education lexicon. The concept of a professional as someone who has time to reflect upon practice, take control of events and manipulate the teaching-and-learning agenda, was swallowed up by a plethora of missives, enforced changes and the imposition of a rigid inspection framework that promoted whole-school conformity. As the end of the millennium approached, primary teachers felt that their professional identity had been undermined by excessive government interference, constant media exposure, uncomplimentary statements by politicians and the corruption of professional accountability into a less palatable 'culpability'. Studies of primary teachers' perceptions of the job at this time were replete with comments about stress, workload, paperwork and innovation fatigue (see, for example, Proctor, 1993; Chaplain, 1995; Campbell, 1996).

With a change of government in May 1997, teachers' expectations were initially high, but they were soon to be disappointed as New Labour, frustrated by 18 years in opposition, burst through the floodgates with a raft of fresh legislation. The Education Secretary, David Blunkett, introduced the catchphrase 'High standards for all' and channelled most of his energies into modifying the culture of primary education, including the establishment of more rigorous pupil testing and timetabled lessons in literacy and numeracy. The other government slogan, 'Teaching: high status, high standards' (DfEE, 1998), proved to be crushingly heavy on the need for high standards and feather-light on the high-status dimension. Accusations of inadequate teaching quality in primary schools, fuelled by questionable inspection evidence, struck at the heart of teachers' professional well-being, as they were told that their best was not good enough and that they either improved or faced the consequences.

As the new century begins, with the government in full flow, education ministers' reputations at stake and a general election still some way off, the reforms continue apace. Countless leaflets and booklets are landing on headteachers' desks from the DfEE and a report in the Times Educational Supplement (7 April 2000) berates the 'barrage of Government documents (and) escalating bureaucratic burden' (p. 6). The bewildering pace of change and centrally imposed regulations continue to impact upon the primary sector, whose reputation to accommodate change has previously been taken for granted. The government holds its collective breath as the vacancy crisis that has hit secondary schools now begins to affect primary schools, and teachers begin to use one of the few weapons they have in their armoury to express their frustration that their professional status is being strangled...voting with their feet. Government ministers swallow hard and battle to redeem the situation by giving eloquent speeches at every opportunity, expressing their (newly discovered) confidence in teachers and the belief that the government's reforms, including the chance to earn more money in exchange for new contractual requirements, will not only restore teachers' confidence but re-establish their sense of professionalism and encourage a new wave of enthusiastic recruits.

The damage to primary teachers' professionalism has bitten deep, however. With the new demands for targeted lessons in ICT, the relentless insistence on year-upon-year improvement in literacy and numeracy, the extension of specialist teaching and the obsession with quantifiable results, the professional transformation from nurturing carer to task-driven attainer has spread to reception and nursery classes. Even the prospect of higher salaries, linked with classroom performance, has done little to alleviate some primary teachers' disdain for a system that has provided new buildings, new resources, new development money, new career structures, new professional development opportunities and new education initiatives, yet has failed to grasp that the professional heart of primary teaching is not reflected in glossy brochures, slick presentation, electronic wizardry or elevated subject knowledge, but in the ability and freedom for teachers to respond to that child's needs in that child's class during that episode in the child's life. Far from raising primary teachers' morale, the plethora of innovations hitting schools around the start of the millennium has brought about what Kane (2000) referred to as 'professional bulimia' as teachers have retreated behind the barricades of reluctant compliance.

Galactic school inspectors landing at the end of the twentieth century who had not visited planet Earth for a few years would have been astonished at the pace and rapidity at which primary professionalism had been wrested away from individual teachers and placed in the hands of politicians. They would have been amazed at central government's controlling interest over education, at the deference of teachers and governors to externally imposed edicts, and at the speed at which different versions of a national curriculum had been introduced with so little consideration about the impact that it would have upon pupils and staff. Our visitors might have pondered the wisdom of introducing league tables of achievement based solely on (limited) measurable outcomes and scratched their antennae as they read the critical tone of government pronouncements about teachers, the loss of some of the more talented and experienced practitioners through ill health and early retirement, and the sudden belated discovery that traditional wisdom, creativity and innovative teaching had some value after all (DfEE, 1999).

As the inspectors filed their report, they would doubtless mention with regret the impact on teacher morale of a crippling and debilitating explosion in paperwork; the mounds of dust-laden files and the long-forgotten publications from government departments languishing in headteachers' filing cabinets across the country; the severity of the inspection framework and the emasculating effects that inspections had made on many governors and teachers (Brimblecombe *et al.*, 1995; Jeffrey and Woods, 1996; Fitz-Gibbon, 1999).

They might well have concluded that professionalism was being defined on the basis of how many initiatives teachers could receive, absorb, interpret, implement and perfect in the shortest possible time. The old heart of professionalism, exemplified by a love of working with children, was being shaken to the core by central imposition. In short, 'Do as we say, in the way we say it, and you will be rewarded; resist our will and you will be disregarded'.

'A funny lot, these earth creatures', the aliens would muse.

As the new millennium unfolds, a growing unease that society is becoming obsessed by measurable outcomes at the expense of other vitally important humanitarian issues is gathering pace. Eisner summarises the position well: 'We need to focus on what is lasting, on what will have its life outside the context of schools' (Eisner, 2000: 349). In fact, obsessive government demands for higher attainment in academic subjects look increasingly insecure as schools move into the twenty-first century. The tragic deaths of several teachers in early 2000, allegedly as the result of unacceptable pressure during school inspections, have shaken the education world. A letter writer to the Education Guardian (11 April 2000) has complained bitterly about 'a continuum of personal anguish and suffering, ranging from sleepless nights and anxiety attacks, through to depression, stress-related illness and premature retirement'. Members of some teaching unions have begun to call for industrial action to signal their hostility to government reforms. The government has begun to introduce payments to PGCE student teachers as an inducement to train. The tide is slowly turning.

Shaping new millennium professionalism

Despite the government stranglehold exerted on the primary school curriculum and teaching methods, teachers in the twenty-first century should still have opportunities to enthuse about learning, encourage children to explore, imagine and fantasise, and present the benefits of cooperation. One element of professionalism will be rooted in the primary teacher's ability to motivate pupils in such a way that the 'three square meals a day' curriculum can be ameliorated by moments of spontaneity, stimulation and unrestrained optimism. A new-millennium professionalism should not only relate to academic progress but reflect the proposition that education is the key to creating a society which is dynamic and productive, and offers opportunity and fairness for everyone (DfEE, 1997), a concept embraced by the term 'citizenship' (QCA, 1998; Holden and Clough, 1998). We do well, therefore, to ponder the extent to which new-millennium professionals should be judged in terms of the values that they bring to the job and the ways in which such ethical and social elements will be incorporated into the fabric of school life. Furlong forcefully describes the teacher's responsibility in this respect: 'Professional practice does involve the utilisation of highly complex forms of knowledge; it also constantly involves teachers in the execution of moral judgements, demanding an explicit recognition of the centrality of values in professional life' (Furlong, 2000: 21). In other words, there needs to be an active commitment towards perceiving the professional role of teachers as including the ability to promote attitudes and actions which contribute towards the common good, rather than individual aggrandisement. If primary teachers are to have any purpose other than to be conduits for predetermined slabs of information, employing predetermined methods and assessed by means of rigid criteria, then the dimension of their professional role that depends upon making delicate classroom decisions in a particular context at a particular moment with particular children must be enhanced. The teacher's professional role as a means by which children are prepared for democratic responsibilities will be even more critical in the future as we face not only economic challenges, but those concerned with the moral fabric of the nation. A country full of highly qualified reprobates is hardly a reassuring prospect.

A new-millennium professional must not only be able to help primary pupils to learn basic skills for life, but also to give them the confidence to face change and handle uncertainty. Craft (1991) draws on work by Costa (1990) in emphasising the significance of helping pupils to think for themselves and be given opportunities to be innovative, creative and risk-takers. Such a teaching approach would emphasise an active rather than a prescribed, passive approach to learning. Problem-solving opportunities and the creation of a learning environment in which risks are encouraged, time constraints on task completion are not arbitrarily imposed, and careful attention is paid to pupils' development, would form the heart of the learning process. An active teaching-and-learning approach of this kind will admit to the sort of uncertainty, variety of possible solutions and longer-term aims that a preoccupation with lesson intentions and learning objectives would never allow.

If new-millennium primary teachers are to grapple with the complexities and diversity of educational provision, presented through information diarrhoea and technological advancement, they need to be people with a sharpened sense of what is desirable and achievable. Conformity to a prescribed model of teaching, without the opportunity to express reservations and explore alternatives, is in danger of producing a body of people whose professionalism is judged less on their aptitude for innovative thought and expression, and more on their willingness to be shaped by their political masters, some of whom may have a short-term commitment to education. The ideal primary teacher for the twenty-first century is, perhaps, someone who can combine the delivery of measurable outcomes with that indefinable capacity to make learning a memorable experience for children. In addition, as testing is now firmly rooted in the education system, teachers should be asking hard questions of those who design and produce tests, especially about their value in improving the quality of teaching and raising standards (Williams and Ryan, 2000). Teachers in the twenty-first century need to be instigators as well as implementers, inquisitors as well as subjects of interrogation, introducers as well as enforcers. The days of passive compliance with the latest government initiative must be replaced by a willingness to inspect the inspectors and combat threats of penalties for non-compliance by presenting well-researched and well-considered arguments for alternatives. If primary teachers of the future are to be anything more than meek recipients of a centrally imposed agenda, they must grit their professional teeth and only accommodate new politically driven directives that are based on sound educational principles.

Professionalism rediscovered

Despite concerted government efforts to disabuse primary teachers of the notion that relationships lie at the heart of their professional life, all the signs point to the fact that altruism dominates their motivation to teach. For instance, Tirri (1999) found that the best interests of the child was the prevalent determinant in the moral dilemmas that teachers in England faced in school. Similarly, Shann (1998), after interviewing 92 middle-school teachers, discovered that their relationship with pupils ranked highest in terms of importance and job satisfaction, and Oberski *et al.*'s study of 43 newly qualified teachers (NQTs) (Oberski *et al.*, 1999) concluded that they were 'not so much motivated by a desire to teach as by a desire to have positive relationships with pupils' (p. 148). A poll by the largest teaching union, the NUT, discovered that 97 per cent of primary teachers considered that working with children was a positive aspect of their job (Mansell, 2000). Katz (1995) summarised the principle well: 'Professions identify the goals of their work with the good of humanity at large' (page 223).

Whatever the future holds, primary teachers need to be free from the grip of anxiety-induced emotional reactions that are 'indicators of an assault on the teachers' sense of professionalism' (Jeffrey and Woods, 1996: 340). While all primary teachers will wish to conform to the public image of a teacher as someone who is trustworthy, intelligent, capable of doing a good job, and generally 'looking the part', central imposition that suffocates them with wave after wave of reforms, initiatives, missives, requirements and threats about the consequences of non-compliance, will undermine the substance of their professionalism. Regardless of the way in which societal norms shift and change, primary teachers are those who, first and foremost, are interested in their pupils and will provide a stable, happy learning environment. In short, happy teachers produce contented pupils who, in turn, produce good results.

If we take for granted the need for primary teachers to behave professionally, the dominant issue concerns the nature of future primary teachers' professional competence. At the time of writing (2000) the trend is towards the sort of professional who has the ability to handle sophisticated technologies and manage a range of teaching assistants who have responsibility for technical support, special needs, pastoral care and the electronic transmission of information, reports and pupil-target promotion. Less account is being taken of teachers' interpersonal skills or relational abilities; the overriding criterion for success is to get the job done efficiently and provide good value for money, monitored through regular teacher appraisal (Montgomery, 1999). Nevertheless, it is to be hoped that a form of professionalism embodied in notions like the Dome Academy remains an illusion, for at the heart of teaching must lie the intimate, indefinable bond between pupil and teacher that creates the conditions for effective learning. Whatever definitions of professionalism are adopted and whatever curriculum changes are initiated, all primary-aged children need opportunities to dream, fantasise, make heroes and grapple with human problems, dilemmas and opportunities. A well-educated young person is not only someone with the ability to read, write and compute, but one who can reason, sympathise, enjoy, celebrate, grieve, create and accept diversity. High standards in academic subjects may spawn selfish egoists or sympathetic benefactors; they can sharpen differences in ability or celebrate all types of success; they can draw a learning community together in mutual support or intensify competitiveness and envy; they can provide equal opportunities for every child or exaggerate the existing disparities. A professional agenda which provides for high academic standards is clearly preferable to one which does not, but there are worrying signs that in the race to turn us into a 'super-nation' of literate giants, our system might be producing moral and spiritual midgets.

Primary teachers of the twenty-first century neglect issues of compassion, caring, mutual cooperation and ethical standards at their peril, as education must encompass both erudition and relationships. A society in which primary-aged children have to be escorted to school and locked up in a security-conscious school building for fear of harm by wicked people is a sign of retrogression, regardless of the academic standards attained. Primary teachers cannot solve all societal ills but they can fight hard to ensure that in the clamour for excellence in school subjects they do not lose sight of the fact that there is more to being a professional than national curriculum test scores and a position in school league tables. It is yet to be proved that the 'high status, high standards' professional, as defined by recent governments, will produce the broad and balanced young people who are our hope for the twenty-first century and beyond.

References

Alexander, R., Rose, J. and Woodhead, C. (1992) Curriculum Organisation and Classroom Practice in Primary Schools: A Discussion Paper, London: Department of Education and Science.

Benford, M. (1998) '1998: Ready for Plowden', Education 3-13, 26:3

Brimblecombe, N., Ormston, M. and Shaw, M. (1995) 'Teachers' perceptions of school inspection: a stressful experience', Cambridge Journal of Education, 25.

Campbell, R. J. (1996) 'Educational reform and primary teachers' work: some sources of conflict', Education 3-13, 24:2.

Central Advisory Council for Education, England (1967) Children and Their Primary Schools, (Plowden Report), London: Her Majesty's Stationery Office.

Chaplain, R. P. (1995) 'Stress and job satisfaction: a study of English primary school teachers', Educational Psychology, 15:4.

Costa, A.L. (1990) 'What human beings do when they behave intelligently and how they can become more so', Curriculum, 11:1.

Craft, A. (1991) 'Thinking skills and the whole curriculum', The Curriculum Journal, 2:2.

Dann, R. and Simco, N. (2000) 'Teachers in charge: a speculative vision of the future of primary education', Education 3-13, 28:1.

DES (1991) The Parents' Charter, London: DES.

DES/Welsh Office (1985) Better Schools, London: Her Majesty's Stationery Office.

DES/Welsh Office (1992) Choice and Diversity, London: Her Majesty's Stationery Office.

DfEE (1997) Excellence in Schools: A Summary, London: DfEE.

DfEE (1998) Teaching: High Status, High Standards, Circular 4/98, London: DfEE.

DfEE (1999) All Our Futures: Creativity, Culture and Education, Sudbury: DfEE Publications.

Eisner, E. W. (2000) 'Those who ignore the past: 12 'easy' lessons for the next millennium', Journal of Curriculum Studies, 32:2.

Farrell, M. (1999) Key Issues for Primary Schools, London: Routledge.

Fitz-Gibbon, C. T. (1999) 'Ofsted is inaccurate and damaging: how did we let it happen?' Forum, 41:1.

Holden, C. and Clough, N. (eds 1998) Children as Citizens: Education for Participation, London: Jessica Kingsley Publications.

Furlong, J. (2000) 'Intuition and the crisis in teacher professionalism', in Atkinson, T. and Claxton, G. (eds) The Intuitive Practitioner, Buckingham: Open University Press.

Jeffrey, B. and Woods, P. (1996) 'Feeling deprofessionalized: the social construction of emotions during an Ofsted inspection', Cambridge Journal of Education, 26.

Kane, I. (2000) 'Paying the Piper: Calling the Tune', Spring Conference, Exeter Society for Curriculum Studies, Exeter, England.

Katz, L.G. (1995) Talks With Teachers of Young Children, Norwood, New Jersey: Ablex Publishing.

Mansell, W. (2000) 'Teachers feel literacy strain', Times Educational Supplement, 7th January 2000.

Montgomery, D. (1999) Teacher Appraisal Through Classroom Observation, London: David Fulton.

Norris, R. (1995) 'Teacher education: continuity, challenge and change', Curriculum, 16:2.

Oberski, I., Ford, K., Higgins, S. and Fisher, P. (1999) 'The importance of relationships in teacher education', Journal of Education for Teaching, 25:2.

Office for Standards in Education (1993) Curriculum Organisation and Classroom Practice in Primary School: A Follow-Up Report, London: Ofsted.

Ozga, J. and Lawn, M. (1981) Teachers' Professionalism and Class, London: Falmer.

Poulson, L. (1998) 'Accountability, teacher professionalism and education reform in England', Teacher Development, 2:3.

Proctor, J. L. (1993) 'Occupational stress among primary teachers: individuals in organizations', Unpublished PhD thesis, University of Aberdeen.

Qualifications and Curriculum Authority (1998) Education for Citizenship and the Teaching of Democracy in Schools, Sudbury: QCA Publications.

Shann, M.H. (1998) 'Professional commitment and satisfaction among teachers in urban middle schools', Journal of Educational Research, 92:2.

Sweetman, J. (1992) Curriculum Confidential Three, Tamworth: Bracken Press.

Tirri, K. (1999) 'Teachers' perceptions of moral dilemmas at school', Journal of Moral Education, 28:1.

Troman, G. (1996) 'The rise of the new professionals? The restructuring of primary teachers' work and professionalism', British Journal of Sociology of Education, 17:4.

Welch, G. and Mahoney, P. (2000) 'The teaching profession' in Docking, J. (ed 2000) New Labour's Policies for Schools: Raising the Standard?' London: David Fulton.

Williams, J. and Ryan, J. (2000) 'National testing and the improvement of classroom teaching: can they co-exist?' British Educational Research Journal, 26:1.

Notes on contributors

Jim Campbell is Director of the Institute of Education at Warwick University. He has been editor of the journal *Education 3-13* and Chair of the Association for the Study of Primary Education. He has written or edited over a hundred articles and books on education. He has a particular research interest in the nature of teachers' work, as exemplified by his two books *Primary Teachers at Work and Secondary Teachers at Work*, both published by Routledge in 1994.

Colin Conner is a former primary and middle-school teacher who now lectures at the University of Cambridge School of Education. His research interests are in the areas of learning, assessment and primary school management. He has published widely in education journals . His two latest books are *Assessment in Action in the Primary School* (Falmer, 1999) and (with Geoff Southworth) *Managing Improving Primary Schools: using evidence-based management for school improvement* (Falmer forthcoming)

Marion Dadds is Professor of Teaching and Learning at St. Martin's College. She has a background in primary education as a class teacher, curriculum coordinator, advisory teacher, in-service tutor and researcher. Her main research, published in a variety of journals, has focused on professional development through various forms of classroom enquiry and action research. Her publications include *Passionate enquiry and school development: a story of teacher action research* (Falmer, 1995)

Marion Dowling is a specialist consultant in early years work. She has been head of a nursery school, an advisory headteacher, an adviser and an HMI. She has written a number of books about early years education, the latest of which is *Young Children's Personal, Social and Emotional Development* (Sage, 1999)

Maurice Galton was formerly Dean of Education at Leicester University. He is now Associate Director of Research at Homerton College Cambridge and Visiting Professor at the Hong Kong Institute of Education. He is best known for his studies of primary classrooms but has also recently studied the impact of transfer from primary to secondary school on pupils' attainment and attitudes. His most recent book is *Inside the Primary Classroom: 20 years on* (Routledge, 1999), a replication of the original ORACLE study.

Denis Hayes is a Reader in Teacher Education at the Rolle School of Education, University of Plymouth. He taught for sixteen years in five different schools before entering teacher education. His research interests include the role of the primary school headteacher, the impact of change, the development of teacher skills in student teachers and the impact of the induction year on new teachers and their tutors. Two of his latest books are *Foundations of Primary Teaching* (second edition, 1999) and *The Handbook for Newly Qualified Teachers* (2000), both published by David Fulton.

Ann Lewis is Professor of Special Education and Educational Psychology at Birmingham University. She was previously a Reader in Education at Warwick University and before that taught in primary and special schools. Her current research interests are in policy analysis and special educational needs and in SEN pedagogy. Her publications include *Researching Children's Perspectives* (with Geoff Lindsay) (Open University Press, 2000), *Primary Special Needs and the National Curriculum* (Routledge, 1991,1995) and *Children's Understanding of Disability* (Routledge, 1995,1999).

Andrew Pollard is Professor of Primary Education at Cambridge University. He was a teacher in Yorkshire primary schools for ten years and has worked in teacher education at Oxford Brookes University, the University of the West of England and the University of Bristol. He has authored many books on primary education including *Reflective Teaching in the Primary School* (Cassell third edition, 1997), *Changing English Primary Schools?* (Cassell, 1994) and *The Social World of Children's Learning* (Cassell, 1996)

Colin Richards is Professor of Education at St. Martin's College, Honorary Professor of Education at the University of Warwick and Visiting Professor at the University of Leicester. He is a former primary school teacher, university lecturer and HMI. He is chair of the National Primary Teacher Education Conference and has been national chair of the Association for the Study of Primary Education. His latest publications include *The Primary Curriculum: past, present and future,* published by Trentham Books in 1999 and *Primary Education: at a hinge of history?* published by Falmer Press the same year. He is currently working on a history of primary education from 1944.

Geoff Southworth is Professor of Education at the University of Reading School of Education and co-director of the School Improvement and Leadership Centre. He was a primary school teacher, deputy headteacher and headteacher before becoming a tutor at the Cambridge Institute of Education. His research interests include primary school improvement, management and leadership and he has also studied primary school cultures and whole-school curriculum development. He has published widely on these topics.

Norman Thomas was a primary teacher and headteacher before becoming an HMI. After retiring as Chief Inspector for Primary and Middle Schools he chaired a committee of enquiry into primary education in the ILEA and acted as specialist adviser to House of Commons select committees. He has been a visiting professor at the Universities of Warwick and Nottingham and is currently visiting professor at the University of Hertfordshire. He has written extensively in professional journals. His own book, *Primary Education from Plowden to the 1990s*, was published by Falmer Press in 1990.

Index